The Nature of Clemson

A Field Guide to the Natural History of Clemson University

by

Lisa K. Wagner, Umit Yilmaz, Victor B. Shelburne, Jerry A. Waldvogel, and Mary Taylor Haque

THIS BOOK IS DEDICATED TO PAST, PRESENT, AND FUTURE MEMBERS OF THE CLEMSON UNIVERSITY FAMILY ENGAGED IN NATURAL RESOURCE CONSERVATION, PRESERVATION, AND EDUCATION IN SOUTH CAROLINA AND THROUGHOUT THE WORLD.

THE BENGAL TIGER: CLEMSON UNIVERSITY MASCOT

As you
approach the
Clemson campus,
you're likely to
encounter large orange paw prints.
Known as the "Tiger Paw", this trademarked paw is the sym-
bol of Clemson athletics, and the emblem was developed from a
real tiger paw print. The Bengal tiger, a carnivore native to Asia,
is Clemson University's mascot. The largest living members of the
cat family, Bengal tigers are strong swimmers and swift run-
ners. Tigers have excellent vision and hunt mostly by stalk-
ing and pouncing at dawn and dusk. Stripes camouflage
them in the shadows of tall grasses, dense thickets, and
riparian habitats. An endangered species, only 3,000
to 7,000 Bengal tigers are thought to still be living
in the wild. Sanctuaries in Asia provide protected habitats including mangrove swamps, dense forests, and savannahs.

Tiger conservation has been a key focus of environmental groups
around the world for decades. Here at Clemson, a Clemson University student organization named "Tigers for Tigers" serves to
increase international awareness and conservation efforts
to save tigers. Clemson students and faculty are also
involved in interdisciplinary teaching,
service, and research activities to
promote wildlife conservation at the local level.

SUPPORT FOR THE DEVELOPMENT OF THIS BOOK WAS PROVIDED BY THE CLEMSON UNIVERSITY INNOVATION FUND, THE SUSTAINABLE UNI-VERSITIES INITIATIVE, AND CLEMSON UNIVERSITY. WE THANK DORIS HELMS FOR HER SUGGESTION OF THE PROJECT.

WE APPRECIATE THE SUPPORT AND INPUT OF OUR COLLEAGUES, ESPECIALLY THE MANY FACULTY AND STAFF MEMBERS WHO HAVE EX-PRESSED INTEREST AND SUPPORT FOR DEVELOPING THE FIELD GUIDE. WE ARE ESPECIALLY APPRECIATIVE OF THOSE WHO 'PREVIEWED' DRAFT COPIES: JENNIFER BAUSMAN, DAVID BRADSHAW, BETH FARMER, TIM SPIRA, AND SHERRY WALDVOGEL. DAVID BRADSHAW, JOE CULIN, STAN-LEE MILLER, ED PIVORUN, AND GREG YARROW PROVIDED HELP WITH IDENTIFICATION. SUE WATTS ASSISTED WITH IMAGE ACQUISITION AND CATALOGING. CHRISTIAN AND DAVE CICIMURRI REVIEWED A FINAL DRAFT OF THE FIELD GUIDE.

HEYWARD DOUGLASS PROVIDED HIS FLYING SKILLS FOR THE AERIAL PHOTOGRAPHS. JIM BARKER GENEROUSLY ALLOWED US TO USE HIS DRAWINGS OF SIKES AND TILLMAN HALLS. CLEMSON UNIVERSITY ATHLETICS PERMITTED USE OF THE TIGER PAW IN A NON-CONVENTIONAL FORMAT. GERALD VANDER MEY AND BARRY ANDERSON IN THE CLEMSON UNIVERSITY CAMPUS PLANNING OFFICE CONTRIBUTED BASE MAPS AND ASSISTANCE WITH NAMES OF CAMPUS AREAS. STEVE CHAPMAN PROVIDED PUBLISHING ADVICE AND PATRICK WRIGHT CONTRIBUTED THE BACK COVER PHOTO OF THE AUTHORS.

PROCEEDS FROM THIS BOOK ARE DEDICATED TO BIODIVERSITY EDUCATION AND SUSTAINABILITY, IN ADDITION TO SUPPORTING CONTIN-UED PRINTING OF THE FIELD GUIDE.

ISBN 978-0-9741516-9-4

Book design and layout by Umit Yilmaz.

Some of this material is based upon work supported by the Cooperative State Research, Education, and Extension Service, U.S. Department of Agriculture, under Agreement No. 2002-38411-12122. Any opinions, findings, conclusions, or recommendations expressed in this publication are those of the authors and do not neces-sarily reflect the view of the U.S. Department of Agriculture.

Published by Clemson University Press, Clemson, South Carolina.

CONTENTS

A Note for 2018
by
Victor Shelburne

This new preface to The Nature of Clemson has CHANGE as its major theme. First, I note that the five authors are all no longer active at Clemson beginning with the untimely passing of Jerry Waldvogel, the retirement of Mary Haque, Vic Shelburne, and Lisa Wagner, and Umit Yilmaz continuing his academic career at the University of Georgia. Although we have chosen not to redo any of the material of The Nature of Clemson produced in 2005, even the most casual observer will note that some of the written details and pictures in the book may be different. Because of the many changes that have occurred on the physical landscape of the Clemson campus over the past 15 years, this re-issued edition offers you, the visitor, parent, student, staff, or faculty member, a unique opportunity to see how the Clemson campus may or may not have changed over time. In other words, embrace the changes that have occurred and challenge yourself to note what has and what has not changed.

Meanwhile, as you walk the campus with this guide, please appreciate the efforts of countless individuals. They blended a setting that matched the natural landscape with the needs of an institution of higher learning and it is our privilege to enjoy the fruits of their labor.

Foreword
by
Doris R. Helms, Ph.D.
Provost

Every day, more than 17,000 students walk across the campus of Clemson University to attend class. While many experience the beauty of campus, many may have also wondered about the identity of a tree or the bird foraging in a nearby shrub.

I am pleased to introduce a book that provides answers for some of these questions and raises other questions with the intention of stimulating dialogue about the outdoor places of this beautiful campus where so many people come to live and learn. The product of a long and ongoing conversation between faculty and students from a variety of disciplines, The Nature of Clemson is the first in what could become a series of field guides showcasing the trees, wildflowers, butterflies, birds, and even buildings that form the backbone of our campus. I hope it inspires readers to search out new and unexplored niches of campus and to link names and knowledge with old familiar sights and sounds. Join the Clemson family in celebrating our natural heritage as you enjoy photos of spring migrants, summer fruit, fall foliage, and winter form depicting the flora and fauna found throughout the changing seasons at Clemson University.

Preface
by
James F. Barker, FAIA
President

SIKES HALL   J. BARKER 9/1/2000

The Nature of Clemson: A Field Guide to the Natural History of Clemson University reveals the unique and memorable natural beauty of the Clemson campus. Faculty, staff and students are what make a University, but the natural and created environment is the setting for our interactions.

Clemson has a beautiful campus, which provides environmental stimulus and opportunity for teaching and learning. This field guide reveals those natural and created settings which allow us to individually discover a true sense of place on the Clemson campus; these outdoor rooms are well remembered as a visitor, student, staff or scholar.

We see the Clemson campus as a garden. To my mind, the campus brings the image of a cultivated place where the craft of the gardener has been applied to former farmland and forest with great effect. In addition to the physical beauty of our campus, we have also created a place of learning, where as teachers, we are "tilling the soil in patterns and with purpose." (Bart Giamatti, former President of Yale University).

I invite you to come and explore the landscape of Clemson University as described in this guide and to learn about how our natural and created world has come together to make this place we call Clemson University.

INTRODUCTION

The Piedmont of South Carolina today is a patchwork of forests, farms, pastures, and developed urban and suburban landscapes.

Clemson University's habitats and natural history reflect similar diversity and history of landscape use, being home to native plants as well as ornamentals, a variety of animals and insects, with layers of history and change reflected in the landscape.

The campus has a significant green framework, an interconnected system of landscape plantings, gardens, creeks, remnant natural areas, and shoreline. These green spaces enrich the lives of our students, faculty, staff, and visitors, offering a green antidote to the increasing pace of urbanization in upstate South Carolina.

Discovering the inhabitants of these green areas on campus enriches our understanding of the environment on which we depend. We hope that this field guide will inspire you to observe and investigate the natural world.

Enjoy using this book as an informal guide as you explore Clemson University's campus.

ABOVE:
The Clemson University campus has a significant green framework which gives it a park-like setting.

BELOW:
A corn snake searches for a meal.

OPPOSITE PAGE:
A historic Eastern red cedar stands in front of Tillman Hall.

flowering dogwood

Carolina wren

T he Clemson University campus reflects much of the urban, suburban and exurban Piedmont today.

The campus also reflects its historic landscape, through its green canopy of native white and red oaks, with traditional horticultural additions of native American holly and its cultivars, red cedar, and river birch.

The 19th century introductions of crepe myrtle, camellia, ginkgo, and nandina are also well-represented on campus, with deodar cedar, liriope, Yoshino cherries, and red maple cultivars adding to the created campus landscape.

Habitat diversity on Clemson University's main campus also reflects the shoreline along Lake Hartwell, once bottomland hardwood forest.

The pockets of forest and woodlands that persist in East Beach (beyond the baseball stadium) and in the South Carolina Botanical Garden provide significant habitat for plants and animals that live in second-growth forests.

The created landscape of lawns, meadows, and roadsides provides additional habitat for many plants and animals adapted to "edges" – or frequently disturbed habitats.

The campus encompasses traditional landscape plantings, designed gardens, and natural area remnants, providing a mosaic of "backyard" wildlife habitats, garden settings, and semi-natural plant communities.

The natural history provided in this guide describes much of what is typical of the Piedmont. Wildlife diversity depends on habitat and species diversity. Areas of particular richness on campus include remnant natural areas, but also include areas that have been intensively planted, such as in the perennial borders and habitat gardens at the South Carolina Botanical Garden.

ABOVE: **ACORNS**
Bur oaks have the largest acorns of any oak species in North America.

LEFT: **CENTENNIAL OAK**
This South Carolina state champion bur oak was designated the centennial oak during Clemson University's one hundredth anniversary celebration.

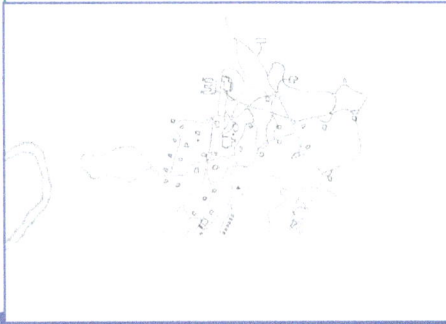

1896

1930

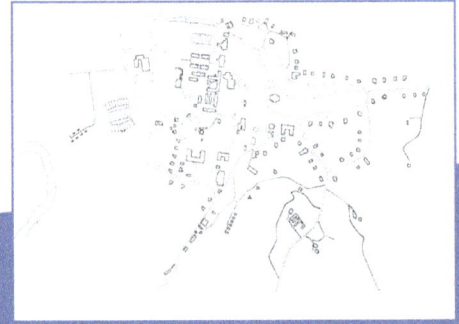

1945

TOP: **CAMPUS MAPS**
Archived maps illustrate campus growth since 1890.

BOTTOM: **TILLMAN HALL IN 1894**
Where cadets used to drill is now Cox Plaza.

The Piedmont hills, flora, and fauna that 18th century naturalist William Bartram lyrically described in his *Travels* had already been shaped by human activity for thousands of years prior to his journey in 1775. In this part of the Piedmont, the Cherokee farmed the river bottoms, used fire to manage the forests and their wildlife, and established trading routes between their 'hilltowns.' A main Cherokee path crossed the Seneca River near where Clemson University is located. Cherokee people still lived here when Bartram journeyed through the Upstate; he describes the town of "Sinica" as being situated on an "extensive fruitful plain" and "Keowe" as "a fertile vale" with "strawberry banks" along the Keowee River. The mixed hardwood forest that Bartram described was probably more open with less underbrush than most of our forests today, due to more frequent fire, even though the Cherokee population was much diminished by then.

Changing river channels and periodic flooding enriched the bottomland soils along the Seneca River. The "bottoms" -- now called the Calhoun Field Laboratory -- is a last remnant of those rich soils, protected by the dike that spared much of Clemson University's historic land holdings from inundation by the filling of Lake Hartwell.

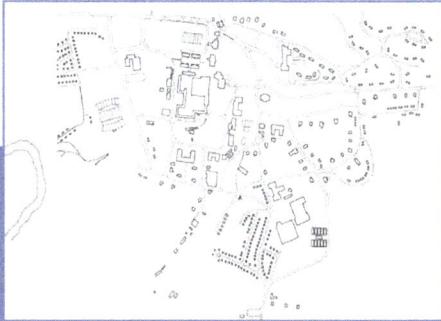

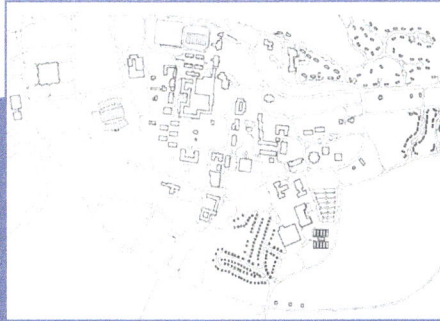

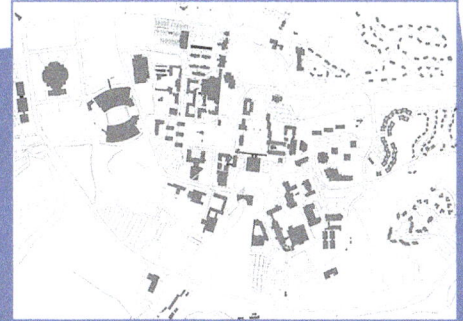

1954   1970   2005

BOTTOM: **TILLMAN HALL IN 2005**
Cox Plaza, between Tillman Hall and Fort Hill, is one of many gathering places on campus.

In the South Carolina backcountry, European settlement flourished after the founding of Pendleton in 1790, with an influx of wealthy families from the lowcountry establishing summer homes and plantations. In 1825, John C. Calhoun, an already well-known political figure and the father-in-law of Thomas Green Clemson, bought a house called Clergy Hall and the surrounding land from the minister of Old Stone Church. He and his wife expanded the house and farm, naming it Fort Hill after Fort Rutledge, which was located nearby.

The plantation, home of Calhoun's daughter Anna Maria Calhoun Clemson and Thomas Green Clemson from 1872 to 1888, became the site of Clemson University when Thomas Green Clemson willed the property to the State of South Carolina to be a "high seminary of learning."

Calhoun and Clemson were both amateur horticulturists and keenly interested in scientific methods of farming. The terraces evident along the Camellia Trail at the South Carolina Botanical Garden are thought to be remnants of the extensive terracing employed to deter erosion at that time.

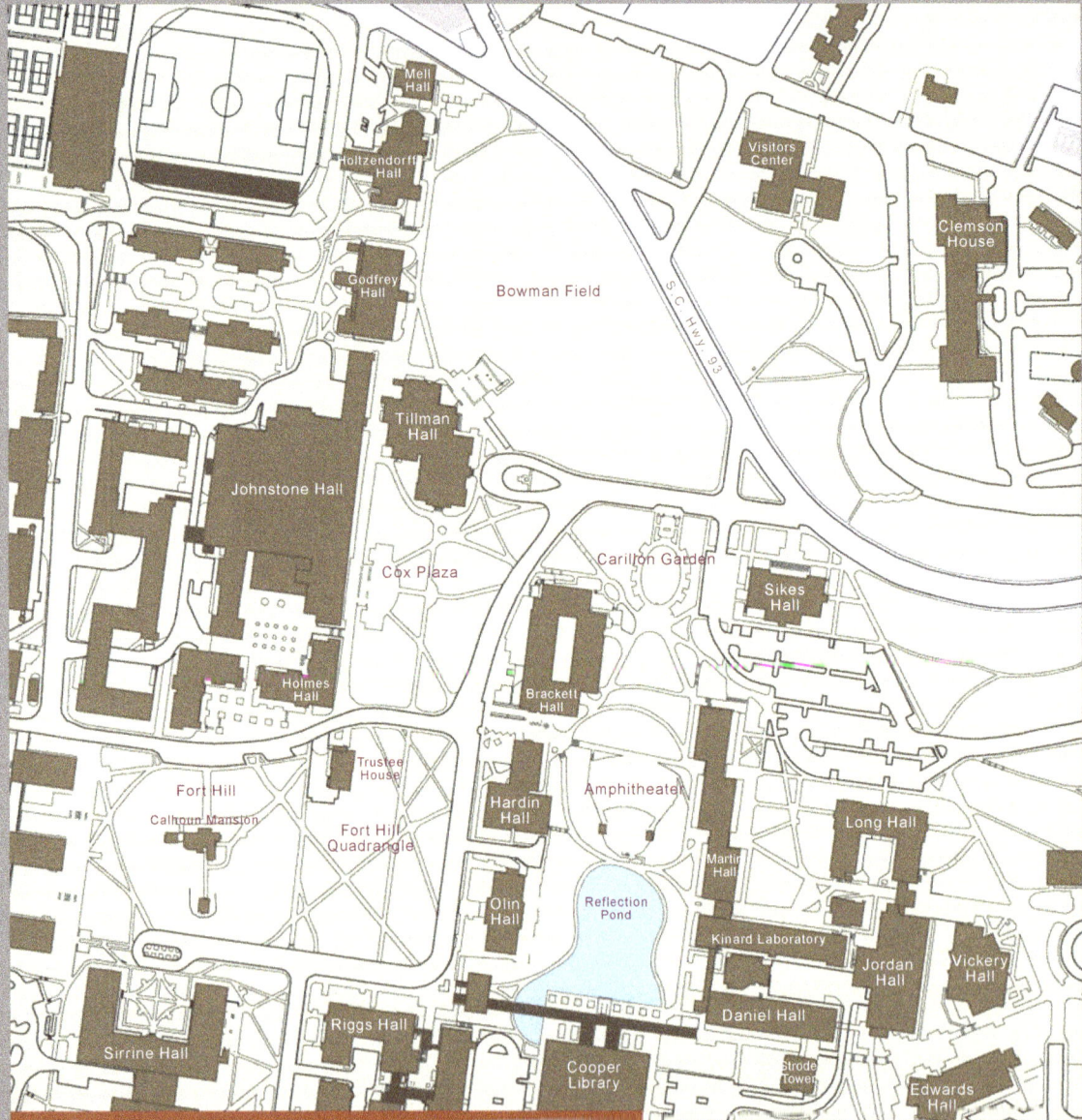

Mell Hall

Holtzendorff Hall

Visitors Center

Clemson House

Godfrey Hall

Bowman Field

S C Hwy 93

Tillman Hall

Johnstone Hall

Cox Plaza

Carillon Garden

Sikes Hall

Holmes Hall

Brackett Hall

Trustee House

Fort Hill

Amphitheater

Calhoun Mansion

Fort Hill Quadrangle

Hardin Hall

Long Hall

Martin Hall

Olin Hall

Reflection Pond

Kinard Laboratory

Jordan Hall

Vickery Hall

Riggs Hall

Daniel Hall

Strode Tower

Sirrine Hall

Cooper Library

Edwards Hall

1/4 MILE, FOUR-MINUTE WALKING DISTANCE: 1,320 FEET

AREA ONE

Bowman Field
Cox Plaza
Fort Hill Grounds
Fort Hill Quadrangle
Carillon Garden
Amphitheater

S tanding near Sikes Hall, it's not hard to imagine the road towards Fort Hill winding along the crest of the hill where Tillman Hall now stands. The 19th century farm became the 20th century college and university campus, with the original 814-acre legacy expanded by additional land to form the main campus. The historic central core campus zone includes many Clemson landmarks – Fort Hill, Tillman Hall, Hardin Hall, and other early academic buildings. Enjoy exploring the area between Bowman Field and Fort Hill Quadrangle, with a side trip to Calhoun Mansion and return via the Cooper Library bridge, passing by the Amphitheater and Brackett Hall, before returning past the Carillon Garden near Sikes Hall.

The green expanse of Bowman Field connects Clemson University's campus to downtown Clemson. It is an intensively managed lawn that today hosts special events, informal gatherings, and serves as a "green beach" on sunny days. The native oaks framing Tillman Hall bore witness to Bowman Field's traditional use as a cadet parade ground and playing field. Oaks native to oak-hickory forests are common on Clemson's campus, including white oak, post oak, red oak, water oak, and willow oak. Large white oaks, post oaks, and red cedars are some of our oldest campus trees, since they're slow growing. The largest have probably seen most if not all of Clemson's history.

ABOVE: **BOWMAN FIELD**
Tillman Hall is the signature building of Clemson University. Large oaks anchor the building, while Bowman Field provides a dramatic foreground.

TOP: **WHITE OAK ACORNS**
White oak acorns germinate rapidly after falling to the ground in fall.

ABOVE LEFT: **WHITE OAK**
The Quadrangle's white oaks were once part of a long allee from Tillman Hall to Riggs Hall.

ABOVE RIGHT: **POST OAK**
The size and spreading branches of the 100-plus year-old post oak reflect this tree's favorable site. Characteristic of dry habitats, this specimen has benefited from abundant water and nutrients.

LEFT: **WILLOW OAK**
Willow oaks are commonly used in landscapes throughout the Southeast because of their adaptability.

RIGHT: **COX PLAZA**
Nandinas surround the bench honoring Walter Cox, former CU president and longtime Dean of Students. Nandinas have been a favorite landscape plant in the South for generations, largely because they're so tough!

When Thomas Green Clemson rode from Pendleton to Fort Hill, he would have followed much the same route as today's travelers. The shape of the massive post oak that stands in front of Godfrey Hall reflects growth in an open woodland and echoes the fire-maintained woodland that pre-dated Fort Hill's development in the early 1800's. The old road from Pendleton to Seneca crossed the river not far from here, following roughly the same path as Highway 93. Can you imagine how the landscape might have looked then, looking down towards the ferry landing?

post oak

Common throughout eastern forests, white oaks have been historically planted as shade trees. White oak leaves are distinguished by their smooth rounded lobes. White oak acorns ripen and fall within one year, and are an extremely attractive food for small mammals and large birds as they're low in tannins. Red oak acorns are richer in fats, but high in tannins; these are the acorns that squirrels usually "store" for winter food.

white oak

red oak

Trees dominate much of Clemson's campus with a mix of changing landscape plantings and natural areas creating the campus landscape. Fire-maintained oak-hickory forest was the original forest cover for much of the Piedmont. Native hollies and other evergreens are used extensively in campus landscape plantings, as are traditional southern plants such as crepe myrtle and liriope. Look for many different species growing around campus, both native and ornamental.

Cox Plaza, with its water oaks, magnolias, and ornamental plantings, is typical of many landscaped areas on campus. Recently-planted white oaks and maples will eventually provide additional habitat for birds and other animals. Look (and listen) for common "backyard" birds in this area. Cardinals, mockingbirds, and blue jays are common year-round residents. Mockingbirds sing most of the year, unlike many of our other birds, whose songs are heard only during their spring breeding season. Mockingbirds continue to add new sounds to their broad song repertoire throughout their lives.

water oak

TOP: **MOCKINGBIRD**
Look for the flash of white tail markings to help identify this common songbird.

BOTTOM: **BLUE JAY**
The raucous call of blue jays is a familiar sound on campus.

LEFT: **HOLLY WITH BERRIES**
Fruits, berries, and seeds provide energy-rich food for birds and other wildlife.

ABOVE: **CAROLINA WREN**
You may have observed the tenacious nest-building behavior of Carolina wrens. The male and female together can build a nest in a matter of days in all sorts of places, including mailboxes and outdoor light fixtures.

BELOW: **CAROLINA CHICKADEE**
The characteristic call of Carolina chickadee sounds like its name – "chickadee, dee, dee"–listen for it in spring and early summer.

ABOVE RIGHT: **WATER OAK**
Water oaks and nandinas are common on campus.

RIGHT: **QUADRANGLE VIEW**
The tree-lined quadrangle lies adjacent to the Trustee House and Fort Hill.

The academic buildings surrounding the quadrangle adjoining Fort Hill are among Clemson University's oldest, including Hardin Hall, the first academic building on campus.

The quadrangle has been planted with white oaks and other species, expanding the historic landscape of Fort Hill. The white oaks and other trees in the quadrangle are favorite areas for Eastern gray squirrels, which are active all year. If you're visiting during fall, watch how actively they collect and bury acorns and hickory nuts. Remarkably, they recover up to 70% of those buried -- in winter, look for signs of the small neat excavations indicating successful recovery.

Squirrels eat more than just acorns and hickory nuts-- they're generalist feeders, and their diet includes fruits, seeds, buds, and flowers of a variety of trees as well as fungi. In spring, neatly snipped tulip poplar flowers on the ground are evidence of squirrel activity! During their breeding seasons in winter and early summer, watch for active courtship and nest-building behavior. A squirrel with a mouthful of leaves or pine needles may be adding material to her winter or summer "drey," a waterproof nest made of twigs, and lined with leaves, moss, lichens or feathers. Eastern gray squirrels also use tree dens, often in an old woodpecker cavity, lined with soft material.

Listen for the call of Carolina wrens in the spring and summer. These adaptable birds nest in many places and sing their familiar "cheerily, cheerily, cheerily" call in many habitats.

Carolina chickadees are also common campus residents; their interest in cavity-excavating for their nests often leads them to softer trunked trees such as river birch.

Large Southern magnolias line the walkway leading towards Fort Hill and beyond. Prized for their large aromatic white flowers and glossy evergreen leaves, they grow well on campus and in the Piedmont, in spite of being native to the Coastal Plain.

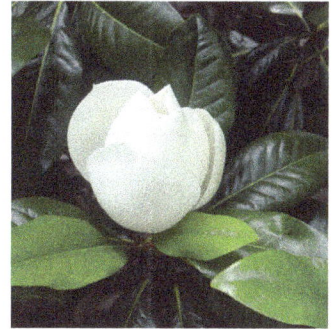

ABOVE LEFT: **HARDIN HALL**
Next to Hardin Hall is a large specimen of Norway spruce, the only hardy ornamental spruce in South Carolina.

TOP: **EASTERN GRAY SQUIRREL**
Squirrels and blue jays, which cache acorns and nuts, are important in regenerating and maintaining second-growth oak-hickory forests.

BOTTOM: **SOUTHERN MAGNOLIA**
Our Southern magnolias are well-traveled – they're desirable landscape plants in mild winter temperate regions of Europe, South America, and Asia.

"…. Four miles from the town (of Pendleton) was his (John C. Calhoun's) famous Fort Hill farm, a splendid property on the Seneca river, with broad acres of bottoms, fertile uplands and forests of native timber."

Dave Sloan, Fogy Days And Now

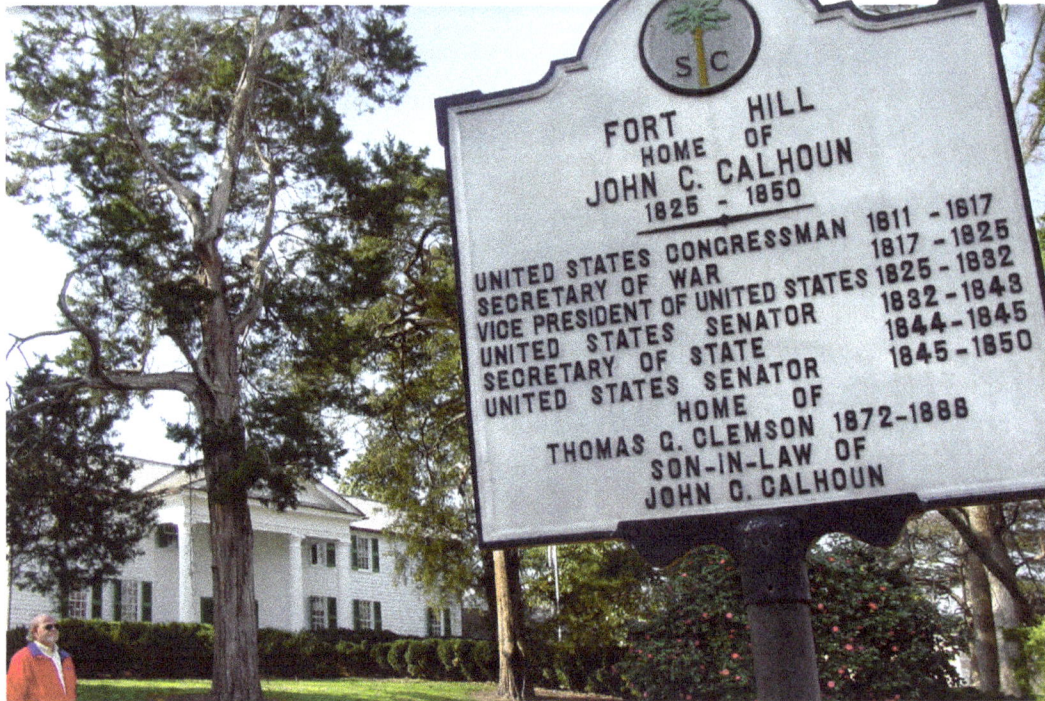

ABOVE RIGHT: **FORT HILL SIGN**
Thomas Green Clemson willed Fort Hill and its surrounding land to the state of South Carolina to be a "high seminary of learning."

ABOVE: **HOME OF J.C. CALHOUN**
From the front porch of Fort Hill, in Calhoun and Clemson's time, there was a clear view of the Seneca River. Today, mature trees, campus buildings, and Memorial Stadium limit the view of Lake Hartwell, but you're still at one of the highest points on campus.

RIGHT: **FORT HILL TODAY**
The trees and shrubs surrounding the old house are a wonderful haven for birds. Depending on the time of year, listen for spring courtship songs, the raucous calling of crows, or the rustling of foraging birds in the trees.

FORT HILL
HOME OF
JOHN C. CALHOUN
1825 - 1850

UNITED STATES CONGRESSMAN 1811 - 1817
SECRETARY OF WAR 1817 - 1825
VICE PRESIDENT OF UNITED STATES 1825 - 1832
UNITED STATES SENATOR 1832 - 1843
SECRETARY OF STATE 1844 - 1845
UNITED STATES SENATOR 1845 - 1850
HOME OF
THOMAS G. CLEMSON 1872-1888
SON-IN-LAW OF
JOHN C. CALHOUN

Spend some time visiting the restored plantation home and explore the grounds surrounding the house. Like many Southern plantation owners, Calhoun was a keen amateur horticulturist. Exchanging memorial gifts of trees and shrubs was an established practice at that time; some of Calhoun's "memory plants" are still evident, including an Oriental arborvitae thought to be a gift of Henry Clay, and the stump of an Eastern hemlock apparently given by Daniel Webster, located near the Trustee Oak memorial. The original Chinese parasol tree in the "rear yard" is attributed to Stephen Decatur; the existing tree is apparently a descendant of that tree.

"... many times have I seen him with his eldest daughter, Miss Anna Maria (later Mrs. Thomas Green Clemson) walking together through the fields and meadows of Fort Hill."

Dave Sloan, Fogy Days And Now

ABOVE: **TRUSTEE OAK MARKER**
This marker commemorates the first meeting of the original seven Life Trustees charged with turning Thomas Green Clemson's vision of a scientific institution on his Fort Hill farm site into reality.

ABOVE LEFT: **ORIENTAL ARBORVITAE**
Oriental arborvitae, native to western China and northern Korea, has been planted in gardens in temperate climates around the world because of its adaptability and drought tolerance. Old specimens like this one are open in appearance; younger trees are bushy.

LEFT: **CHINESE PARASOL TREE**
The Chinese parasol tree in the "rear yard" is showy in spring, here shown in its winter leafless form.

deodar cedar

GRAY CATBIRD

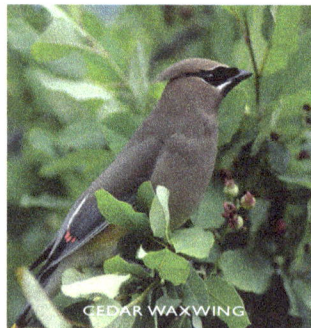

CEDAR WAXWING

BROWN THRASHER

ABOVE RIGHT: **DEODAR CEDARS**
The large deodar cedars near Sirrine Hall were added to the Fort Hill grounds in the 1930's to replace red cedars removed in Sirrine's construction.

RIGHT: **RED CEDARS**
Calhoun planted many other trees, including the red cedars along the entrance drive and plantation road. Slow-growing, these venerable trees were probably planted in the 1840's.

The fleshy cones of Eastern red cedar provide food for many species of birds, including mockingbirds, brown thrashers, cedar waxwings, and gray catbirds. Red cedar's evergreen foliage also provides protection for nesting songbirds.

ABOVE : **CAMELLIA**
Camellias arrived in America late in the 17th century and rapidly became popular throughout the South. Long-lived, large camellias are often quite old. Look for lichens on their bark!

LEFT: **PORT ORFORD CEDARS**
The pair of Port Orford cedars that frame the Trustee House are the only representatives of this species on campus. Native to the Northwest, there are numerous cultivars used as ornamentals.

RIGHT: **GINKGOS**
Ginkgo biloba is a living fossil, the last surviving species of a once-common plant family, with a history dating back over 200 million years. Fossilized Ginkgo leaves have been found in North America, indicating it once grew here. It was reintroduced to the U.S. as an ornamental in the late 1700's. Look for ginkgos planted throughout campus.

TOP: **REFLECTION POND**
The pond north of Cooper library serves as a reflecting pond.

ABOVE: **AMPHITHEATER**
The Outdoor Theater was a gift of the Class of 1915 and the federal government through the WPA. Built-in fountains were part of the original construction, although they do not operate today.

RIGHT: **RIVER BIRCH & VIEW FROM QUADRANGLE TOWARDS BRIDGE**
From the vantage point of the bridge, look for soaring hawks or turkey vultures above the horizon. It's also a good place to watch for mixed-species flocks of birds moving across campus.

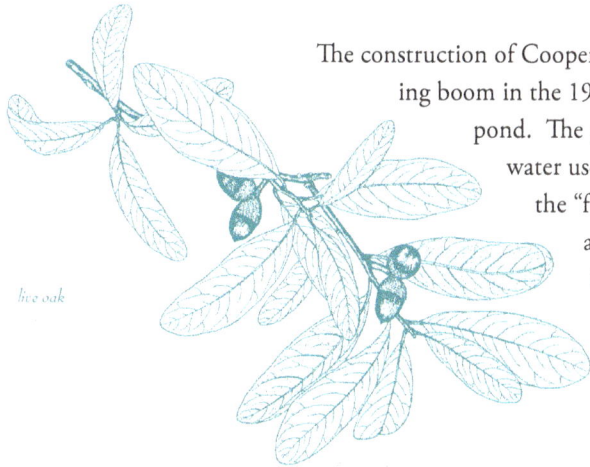

The construction of Cooper Library, during Clemson University's building boom in the 1960's, preceded development of the bridge and pond. The pond in front of the library serves to cool the water used in campus heating and cooling systems, so the "fountains" run intermittently. Located in an area that was once an old creek draw, the pond is edged with large river birches, laurel oaks, and live oaks. The semi-evergreen leaves of laurel oak and the evergreen ones of live oak support a diversity of insects, a boon to insect-eating birds.

Look for the live oak directly adjacent to the library side of the bridge – there's a canopy-level view of the upper branches and leaves of this coastal species.

live oak

TOP: **COOPER LIBRARY**
The roof of the Strom Thurmond Institute serves as a plaza on the south side of Cooper Library.

ABOVE: **COOPER LIBRARY UNDER CONSTRUCTION**
Cooper Library was built in the early 1960's, during Robert Edwards' long tenure as Clemson University's president.

LEFT: **LIVE OAK**
Live oak leaves are recognizable by their thick, leathery texture, glossy surface, and slightly curled edges.

RIGHT: **CATKINS**
Oaks have separate clusters of male and female flowers on the same tree. In spring, wind blows pollen from the catkins (male flowers) to the petal-less female flowers, which produce fruits (the acorns).

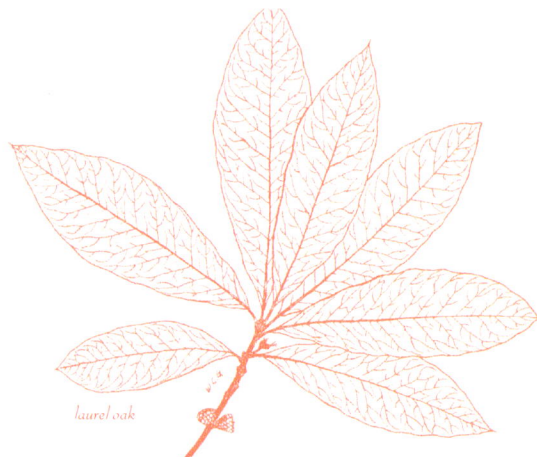

laurel oak

TOP: **RED-BELLIED WOODPECKER**
Red-bellied and other woodpeckers cache acorns, nuts, and insects in bark crevices and cavities. In fact, acorns make up 10-20% of their diet in fall and winter. Listen for the tapping, drumming and calling of males during courtship.

RIGHT AND ABOVE: **LAUREL OAK**
Commonly used in landscaping, laurel oaks are native to the south-eastern Coastal Plain. Their abundant small acorns are important wildlife food, favored by squirrels, blue jays, and red-headed wood-peckers, among other species.

BOTTOM: **WHITE-FOOTED MOUSE**
Abundant in a variety of habitats, white-footed mice eat seeds and nuts, small fruits and berries and some insects.

TOP: AMERICAN ROBIN
In late winter and early spring, watch for flocks of robins devouring any remaining berries or other fruits on trees and shrubs.

ABOVE LEFT: LARGE WHITE OAK NEAR BRACKETT HALL
The older white oaks on campus are increasingly vulnerable to old age and soil compaction through foot traffic and parking.

ABOVE RIGHT: LANDSCAPED STEPS NEAR MARTIN HALL
There's not much visible evidence of the old streambed near the steps connecting the Sikes Hall parking area to Martin Hall and the amphitheater (and into the cooling pond). The creek channel, now "underground," has continued to provide challenges to Clemson University facility managers over the years. It's not hard to imagine that water once flowed here, judging from the slope of the land!

LEFT: CARILLON GARDEN
This area has continued to change over the years. Early photos showed cadets lined up on lawn and bare soil, with Tillman Hall as the backdrop.

Sirrine Hall

Riggs Hall

Daniel Hall

Fernow
Street
Cafe

Hunter
Laboratory

Cooper
Library

Freeman
Hall

Earle
Hall

Campus
Green

Fluor Daniel
Building

Lowry
Hall

Lowry
Courtyard

Thurmond
Institute

Lee
Courtyard

Barre Hall

Lee Hall

Lehotsky
Hall

Brooks
Center

Suber Pond and
Waterfall

Brooks Center Woods

Tiger Band
Practice Field

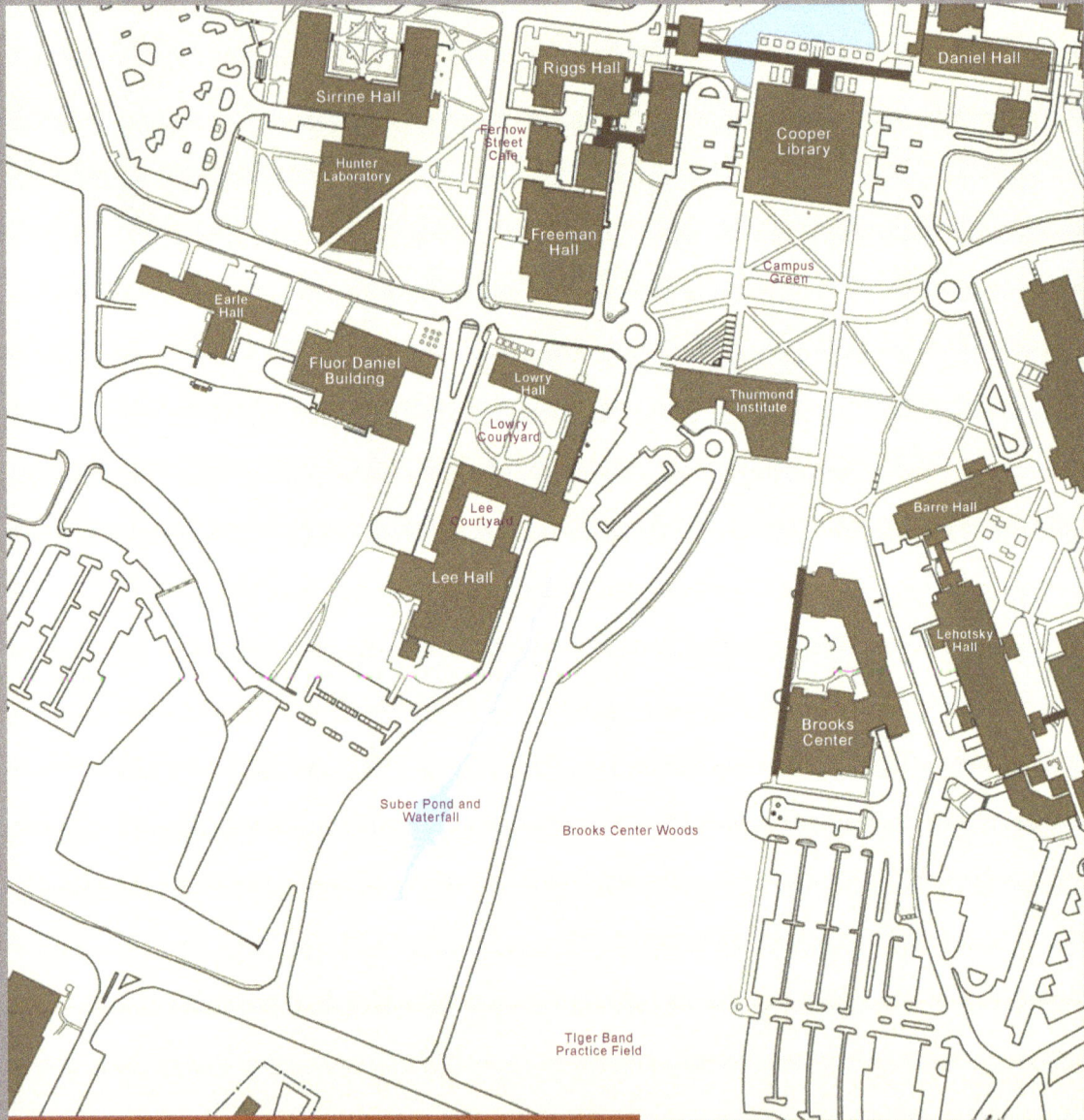

1/4 MILE, FOUR-MINUTE WALKING DISTANCE: 1,320 FEET

AREA TWO

Brooks Center Woods
South of Cooper Library
Strom Thurmond Institute
Lee Hall

The dark pink and almost red flowers of redbud trees frame the campus and library in the spring as you walk between McGinty Mall and the Brooks Center. Look for the redbud flowers before the leaves emerge. Redbuds are actually members of the bean family and you might notice the persistent pods on the branches of the tree. Its heart-shaped leaves distinguish it during the growing season.

The whole Brooks Center complex and fields were once home to the small apartments known as the "prefabs," married student housing erected after World War II to accommodate married servicemen attending Clemson. By the early 1980's, they had definitely outlived their usefulness! The large field in front of the Brooks Center stands in contrast to the oak woods to the south. This open park of old post oaks, southern red oaks, white oaks, and black oaks still gets a lot of use. These are all mostly dry site species that you will find on the top of the typical hill in the Piedmont. Their generally large size indicates that this area has been fairly well-protected for the last 100 years. The Clemson band practices on the far side, so these trees get a full dose of music at least twice a week in the fall. Also, numerous classes in forestry and horticulture use the park-like setting as an outdoor classroom.

TOP: **REDBUDS**
Redbuds in bloom frame the Cooper Library.

BOTTOM: **FORMER HOUSING**
The "prefabs" were a common sight around campus until their demise in the early 1980's.

TOP: **CATALPA FRUIT**
The Southern catalpa tree produces distinctive cigar-like fruits.

ABOVE RIGHT: **BROOKS CENTER**
The woods near the Brooks Center include a variety of native trees.

RIGHT: **SOUTHERN CATALPA**
Look for the whorled leaves of the Southern catalpa or "fishbait" tree.

LEFT: **MOCKERNUT HICKORY**
Mockernut hickories have 3-7 fragrant leaflets and thickly husked fruits.

mockernut hickory

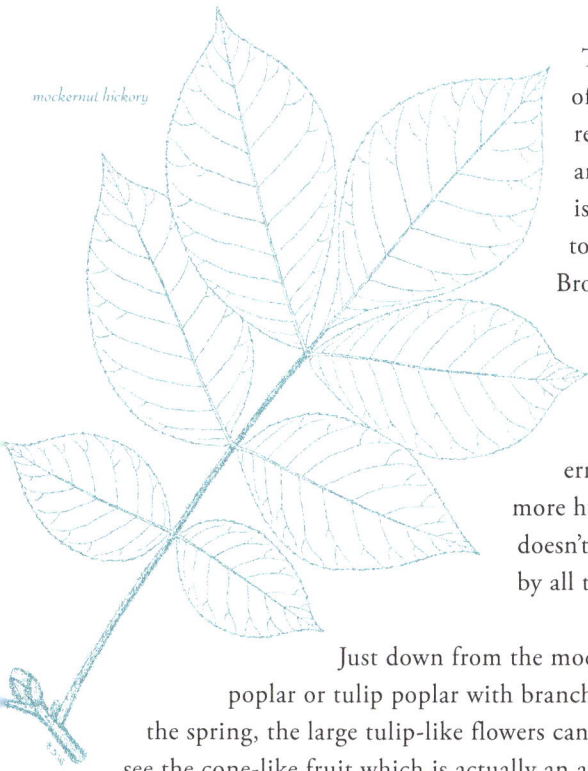

The hickory trees on campus are a great source of nuts for our campus population of squirrels. Pignut and mockernut are found on drier areas of the campus while the bitternut hickory is found along our campus streams and bottoms. One particular mockernut hickory in the Brooks Center woods has low-hanging branches making the large nuts easy to reach in the fall. But try to pry one open or even better yet, try to get to the meat of the nut and you will soon learn why it is called "mockernut." Although a sweet hickory nut, there is more husk and woody covering than there is seed. It doesn't seem to deter the squirrels, however, judging by all the chewed nuts on the ground.

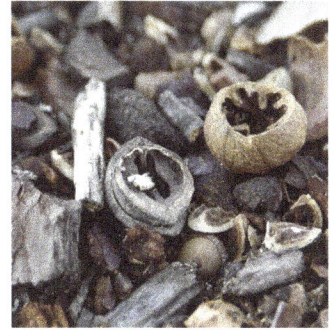

Just down from the mockernut hickory is a large, open-grown yellow poplar or tulip poplar with branches that can be reached from the ground. In the spring, the large tulip-like flowers can be inspected up close and in the fall, you can see the cone-like fruit which is actually an aggregate of many seeds all clustered together. One of the tallest trees in the eastern United States, its distinctive square leaves make this tree easy to identify.

catalpa leaf and fruit

Above the road to the Strom Thurmond Institute, look for the trees with very large yellow-green leaves in whorls of three that distinguish the Southern catalpa tree. Another common name for catalpa is "cigar-tree" named after the elongated cigar-like fruit which hangs from the tree in the fall. These fruits are the product of a huge pyramid of snapdragon-like flowers that bloom each spring. Yet another common name is fishbait tree, for the catalpa worm or caterpillar which feeds exclusively on this tree and grows to 4 inches in length. Prized by anglers, these caterpillars can completely strip a tree of its leaves in the summer.

TOP: **CHEWED HICKORY NUTS**
Squirrels feast on the hickory nuts found throughout campus.

BOTTOM: **YELLOW POPLAR OR TULIP POPLAR**
Yellow poplar blooms abound in late April with tulip-like flowers for which the tree is also named tulip poplar.

catalpa sphinx caterpillar

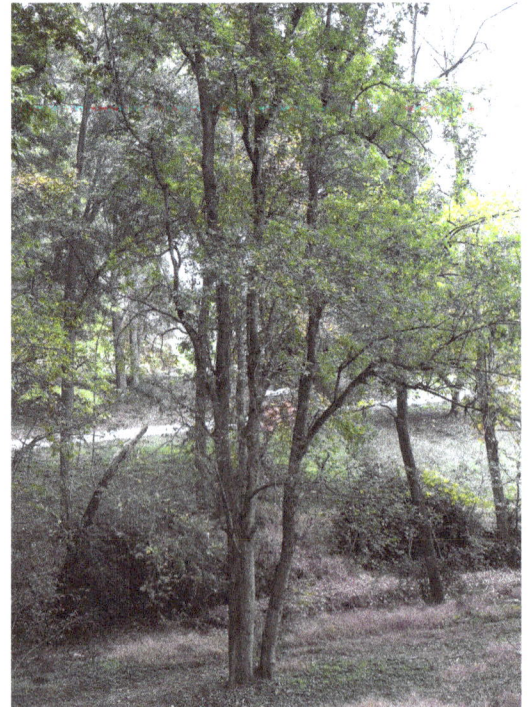

TOP: **BRIDGE**
This pedestrian bridge spans Suber Pond.

BOTTOM: **SQUIRREL TRACKS**
A rare snowy scene of the bridge reveals the tell-tale track of a squirrel checking food stores.

ABOVE RIGHT: **SUBER POND**
The small pond and creek below the Brooks Center provide habitat for crayfish and other aquatic organisms.

RIGHT: **BOXELDER**
Moisture-loving boxelders are common along streams on campus and throughout the Piedmont.

Below the Brooks Center woods is a lovely pastoral area of campus. The stream that went underground at the cooling pond re-emerges and begins its short journey to Lake Hartwell. A small duckpond built many years ago graces this ravine and bridges provide access. Large water-loving sycamores, boxelders, river birches, and black willows adorn the stream bank. Come down here on fall afternoons and you will be serenaded by the Clemson band.

A venerable old American beech tree stands like a sentinel above the stream bank on the far side. Large roots cascade down over the bank making the tree look almost as if it would like to take a walk. The smooth elephant-grey bark has seen a lot of Clemson history and, in this case, the history of former love affairs is written in the compliant bark. This particular tree is over 11 feet in circumference and 90 feet tall. Years of protection on the campus have undoubtedly led to its record size.

sycamore

river birch

ABOVE & LEFT: **AMERICAN BEECH**
The massive trunk of this venerable American beech makes it one of the largest in South Carolina.

TOP: **SOURWOOD FLOWERS**
Sourwood flowers attract local bees in early summer.

ABOVE MIDDLE: **SOURWOOD**
Sourwoods in the courtyard of Lee Hall exhibit the distinctive irregular branching pattern typical of this species.

ABOVE RIGHT: **SWEETGUM**
Star-shaped sweetgum leaves and their spiked fruits are a common sight on campus.

RIGHT: **SIRRINE HALL & CHINESE ELM**
This massive Chinese elm exhibits the flaky orange bark characteristic of this species.

sweetgum

Look for the large sweetgum if you're in the vicinity of Lee Hall. A fairly common tree on campus, sweetgums have spiky fruits that can be a hazard to those who insist on walking with bare feet. The one-inch round fruit is the result of numerous flowers fused together. Although sweetgum does best in moist areas, it's frequently found in the upland areas and along roads where it gets plenty of sun. The leaves are known for their burgundy fall color.

In the Lee Hall courtyard, amidst the landscape plantings is a sourwood, which judging by its size, may have been there before the buildings were built. Also, as a shade-loving species, we can assume it was surrounded by woods before the buildings were built. Sourwoods bloom in early summer with thousands of little white flowers, reminiscent of lily of the valley flowers in arrangement. Even in the winter you can see the previous year's fruit high up in the tree arranged on pendulous sprays. Sourwood flowers are actively worked by honeybees, producing excellent light honey.

white pine

Near the entrance to the Sirrine Courtyard is a deodar cedar, a species native to the Himalayan mountains. While our native pines, such as white pine, have needles in bundles, the deodar cedar has shorter green needles mostly born singly on spur shoots. Instead of cones that are pendant and fall intact as in our native pines, the cones of the true cedars are born upright and appear like barrels. You won't find any cedar cones on the ground, however; these cones disintegrate on the tree, thereby spreading their seeds and scales.

In the Sirrine Hall courtyard are large Chinese elms, or lacebark elms. The gracefully ascending branches are reminiscent of our own American elm, which has been ravaged by Dutch elm disease. The distinctive feature on this tree is the bark which peels and leaves orange flecks all over the trunk. A combination of resistance to Dutch elm disease, unique bark, and resistance to urban pollution have made this a favorite for planting on the campus, although they can be weedy. Highway 93 medians on both the east and west approaches to campus feature plantings of these trees.

TOP: **GOLDFINCH**
American goldfinches are commonly found foraging in grassy meadows.

BOTTOM: **DEODAR CEDAR**
The non-native deodar cedar from the Himalayas is a common ornamental on campus.

LEFT: **CHINESE ELM**
Look for the flaking bark characteristic of older Chinese elms!

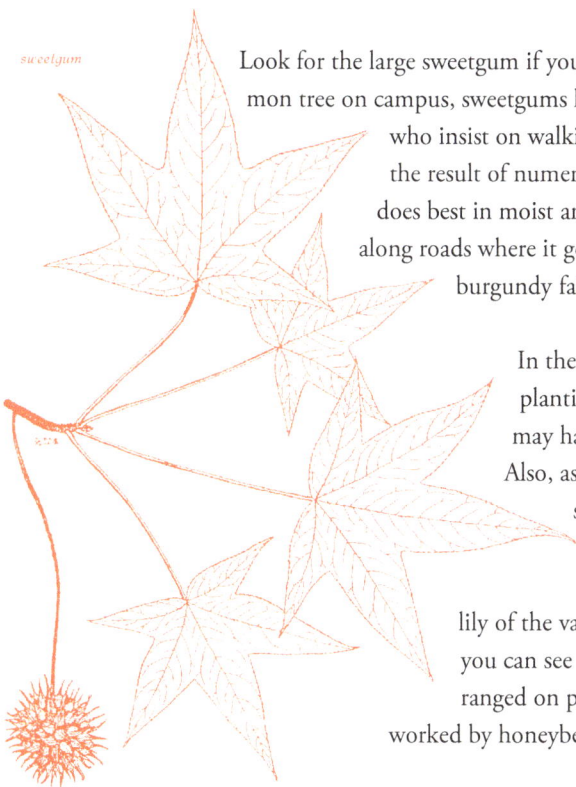

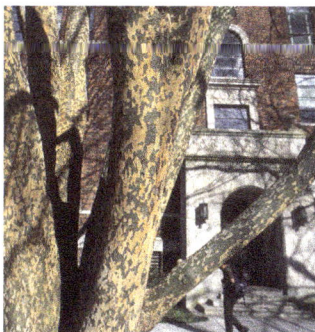

Strode
Tower

Edwards
Hall

Schilletter
Dining Hall

Lever
Hall

Hendrix Student
Center

Redfern
Health
Center

McAdams
Hall

Centennial
Oak

Barre
Hall

McGinty
Mall

Newman
Hall

Biosystems Research
Complex

Lehotsky
Hall

Poole Agricultural
Center

Upper Branch of
Hunnicutt Creek

Greenhouses

Hunnicutt Creek
Riparian Area

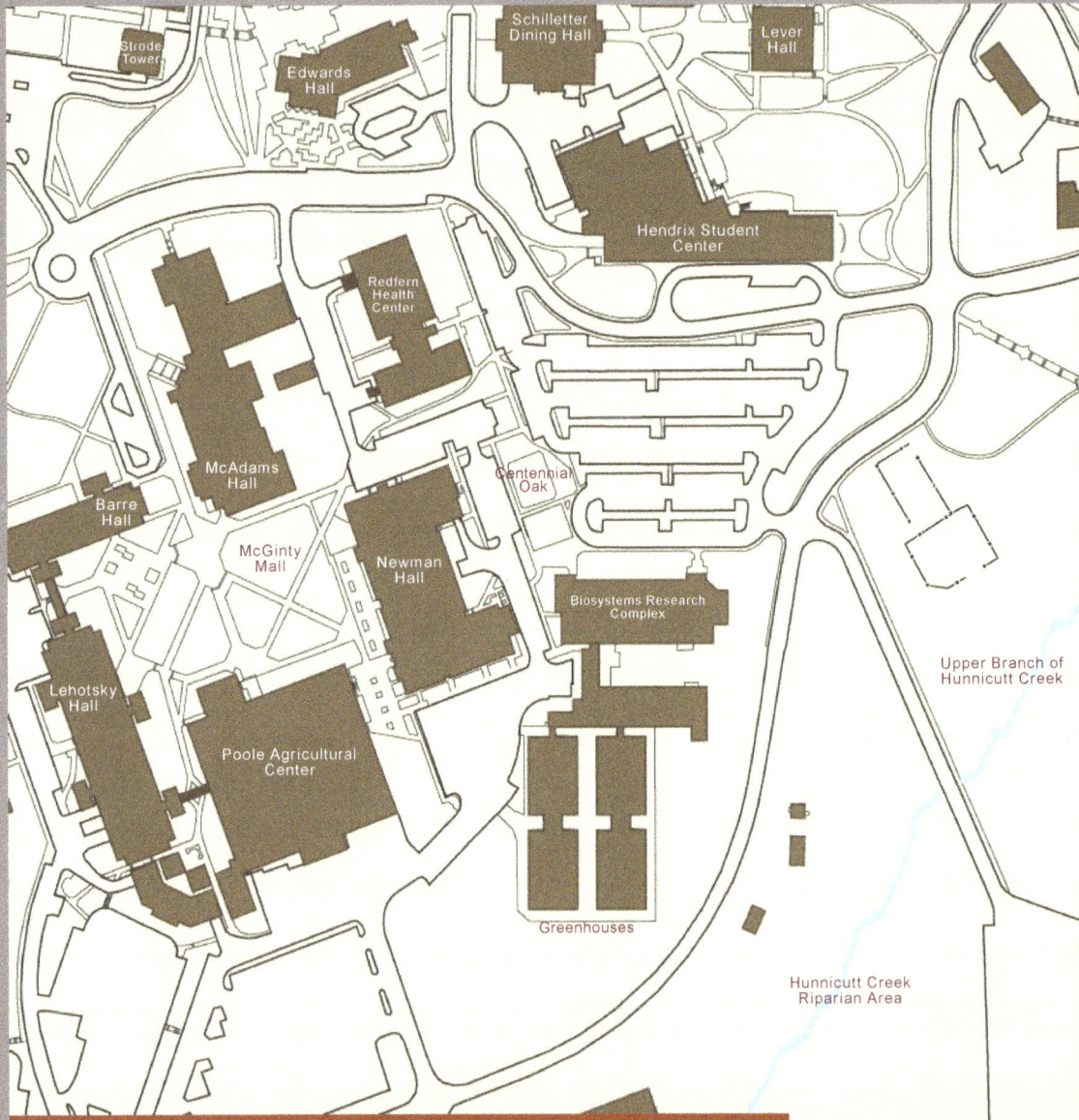

1/4 MILE, FOUR-MINUTE WALKING DISTANCE: 1,320 FEET

AREA THREE

McGinty Mall

Note as you look down the sidewalk towards the core campus how the Tillman Hall bell tower serves as a campus landmark and provides a focal point to students as they head back to the main campus.

The long row of crepe myrtles in front of McAdams Hall heralds your approach into the McGinty Mall area where many of the traditional agriculture and forestry departments are located. Expansion of the campus in the post World War II era pushed these traditional programs away from the core campus area. The resulting landscape is now a hodge-podge of existing native species and planted ornamentals.

The "front lawn" area of Barre Hall and opposite McAdams Hall is a haven for many species of maples. A silver maple at the corner of McAdams Hall is recognized by the obvious silver-colored leaves. A relatively weak wood, however, makes this species susceptible to wind damage, and we find little of it on campus. In contrast, the native red maple is probably one of the most common trees on campus because it is so adapted to a wide variety of sites. Two other species of non-native maples are found here: the black and sugar maples. To some botanists, they are just varieties of the well-known sugar maple, but others insist on separating them by the darker bark and leaves that droop more on the black maple. Whatever the distinction, they are both producers of quality maple syrup in their native northern habitat where cold spring nights and warm days stimulate the production of the sugary sap.

red maple

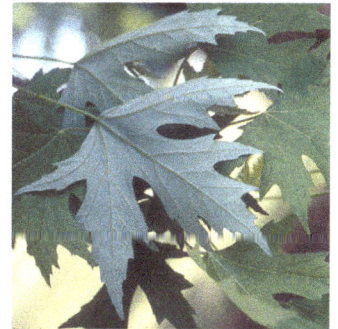

ABOVE: **SILVER MAPLE LEAVES**
When winds blow, the bright backside of the silver maple leaves show off.

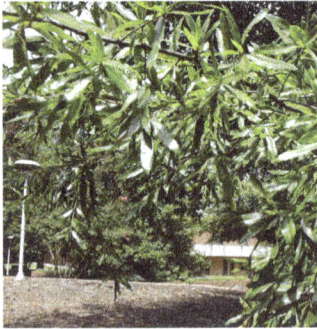

TOP: **ROBBER FLY**
Predaceous on a variety of insects, this beneficial robber fly should be encouraged.

BOTTOM: **WILLOW OAK**
The willow oak is one of our fastest growing oaks and is associated with moister sites.

ABOVE RIGHT: **MCGINTY MALL**
This beech and the deciduous oaks in McGinty Mall provide shade in summer and allow sunlight in winter.

LEFT: **VIEW FROM MCGINTY MALL**
Tillman Hall is visible as students head away from McGinty Mall, flanked by crepe myrtles and willow oaks.

RIGHT: **WILLOW**
A young weeping willow complements one of a series of sculptures designed by John Acorn.

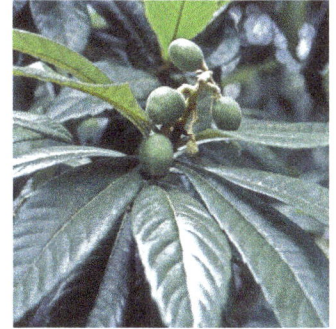

In McGinty Mall, notice the variety of common campus tree species: white and willow oaks, a few southern magnolias and pecans near Lehotsky Hall. Early photographs of this area show just a few small trees. But fertilizer and a lack of competition have now produced a virtual forest. These oaks provide excellent nesting habitat for the gray squirrel.

Look for the Japanese loquat at the main entrance to the Poole Agricultural Center. A subtropical species, loquats can survive down to 10 degrees Fahrenheit. Note that the tree is in the corner of two walls which provide protection from wind and some radiating heat on those cold winter nights. The loquat is a beautiful evergreen tree and makes an excellent ornamental for the garden.

TOP: **JAPANESE LOQUAT FRUITS**
The fruit can be eaten fresh from the tree and frozen for later use to make excellent jelly, jam, preserves and pies, but cold weather prevents fruit ripening on this specimen.

ABOVE LEFT: **WHITE OAK LEAVES**
The distinctive rounded lobes of white oak distinguish a common tree on McGinty Mall.

ABOVE MIDDLE: **SOUTHERN MAGNOLIA**
Creamy white magnolia flowers develop into large cone-like fruits.

ABOVE RIGHT: **GRAY SQUIRRELS**
Squirrels find excellent nesting and foraging habitat on campus.

LEFT: **CREPE MYRTLE**
The crepe myrtle, native to Asia, is one of the few trees that we can count on to bloom heavily and profusely in the hot summer months of July and August. If pruned properly, it has a sculptured winter form with multiple trunks.

RIGHT: **JAPANESE LOQUAT TREE**
Cloaked in a dusting of snow but protected from winter winds, this loquat's microclimate enables it to survive cold winters.

TOP: **RIVER BIRCH**

River birches are prized as ornamentals because of their habit of multiple trunks and flaky bark. Although a tree that prefers a wet environment, it does well as an ornamental. Planted along the west side of Newman Hall, these deciduous trees provide shade on the building in the summer and allow sun to warm the building in winter, making Newman Hall much more energy efficient.

ABOVE RIGHT: **NEWMAN HALL**

River birch and ginkgo frame the Newman Hall courtyard.

RIGHT: **CENTENNIAL OAK**

The spreading horizontal branches of the Centennial bur oak remind us of the live oak. This is the South Carolina State Champion bur oak.

Ginkgos are a common ornamental on the Clemson campus. Native to China, ginkgos are no longer found anywhere in their native habitat. In fact, it is hypothesized that without the planting of this species in Buddhist temples and gardens, it would otherwise be extinct. Despite the small fan-shaped broad leaves, this species is actually more closely related to pines than the oaks in the area. Each tree, like our native American holly, is either male or female. The cones of this species, about one inch across, have a ghastly odor when they ripen and fall on the ground to rot. Despite this drawback, the graceful limbs with their stout spurs and tufts of leaves make for an interesting contrast to the other trees in the area. In fall, we are rewarded with the deep golden-colored leaves. Just watch where you step in the fall!

ginkgo leaves and fleshy cones

A large bur oak was designated the centennial oak during Clemson University's 100th anniversary celebration. The tree's size made it a good guess that it had been around since the founding of the University in 1889. Imagine what it has seen. When it was first planted, it was far away from the campus center. In addition, we know it was planted because this species is not native to South Carolina. The concrete planter which surrounds it was probably added during the construction of Newman Hall and the parking lots. This is the most massive tree on the Clemson campus and is the State record for this species (see www.clemson.edu/champtree for a complete listing of all champion trees in the State).

Bur oak has the largest acorns of any oak species in North America, but you'll have trouble finding one on this tree. Years of drought and stress have limited its allocation of resources to produce seed. History is unclear as to who planted the bur oak and why so far from the main campus. Was it C. C. Newman, Horticulturist and Professor who worked at Clemson from 1905 until his death in 1946? He is credited for having maintained many of the trees on campus and it is entirely possible that he planted it near where a building was eventually named after him. The only problem with this theory is that it would not have been 100 years old in 1989. So did we guess wrong? The answer will be forthcoming the day it finally falls and we can count the growth rings.

bur oak acorns

TOP: **GINKGO LEAVES**
The small fan-shaped leaves of the ginkgo are borne together in a spur shoot.

BOTTOM: **RESURRECTION FERN**
Notice the resurrection ferns growing on the branches of the Centennial oak. The rhizomes of this delicate fern take "root" in the bark and get whatever nutrition they can from rain water. They rehydrate when it rains and dry out almost completely in dry weather.

LEFT: **BUR OAK**
A recently planted bur oak now stands between Lehotsky and Barre Halls. Try to imagine what this area might look like in the future when this small tree grows to the size of the "centennial oak" near Newman Hall.

TOP: **CHERRY FLOWERS**
Yoshino cherry flowers are a short-lived, but spectacular spring sight.

ABOVE RIGHT: **YOSHINO CHERRIES**
Yoshino cherry trees grace the aptly named Cherry Road. The same species surround Washington, D.C.'s Tidal Basin.

RIGHT: **CHERRY TREE IN FLOWER**
Okame cherries are prized as ornamentals; this species is similar to Yoshino cherry in appearance.

Cherry Road is well-named due to the numerous Yoshino cherries planted along it and in the parking lot of the Poole Agricultural Center. A naturally-occurring hybrid of two native Japanese cherries, the tree is noted for its profusion of light pink blooms which usually open in late March each year. When the flowers begin to break apart, the millions of petals look like snow falling and cover the area in a pink carpet. This same species is celebrated during the Cherry Blossom Festival in Washington, D.C.

tiger swallowtail

Near the Lehotsky/Poole breezeway, a small created landscape benefits from the sound of a curtain-like waterfall from the water cooling plant that chills the water for this part of campus. A butterfly garden with butterfly bush, daylilies, daffodils, and yarrow surrounds this little oasis.

Leyland cypress, a serendipitous cross between Alaska yellow-cedar and Monterey cypress, provides great cover for birds such as mourning doves and cardinals. Planted extensively throughout the southern United States, they are usually sterile and produce no edible seeds for wildlife. They are, however, easy to propagate by cuttings from the young branches.

TOP: **MOURNING DOVE**
Watch for mourning doves perched on telephone wires and listen for their distinctive call.

ABOVE: **MALE CARDINAL**
Cardinals are common year-round residents in South Carolina.

LEFT: **BUTTERFLY GARDEN**
The sitting area between Lehotsky and Poole provides a respite for many faculty and students.

RIGHT: **LEYLAND CYPRESS**
The pair of Leyland cypress in front of Lehotsky Hall provide habitat for campus birds.

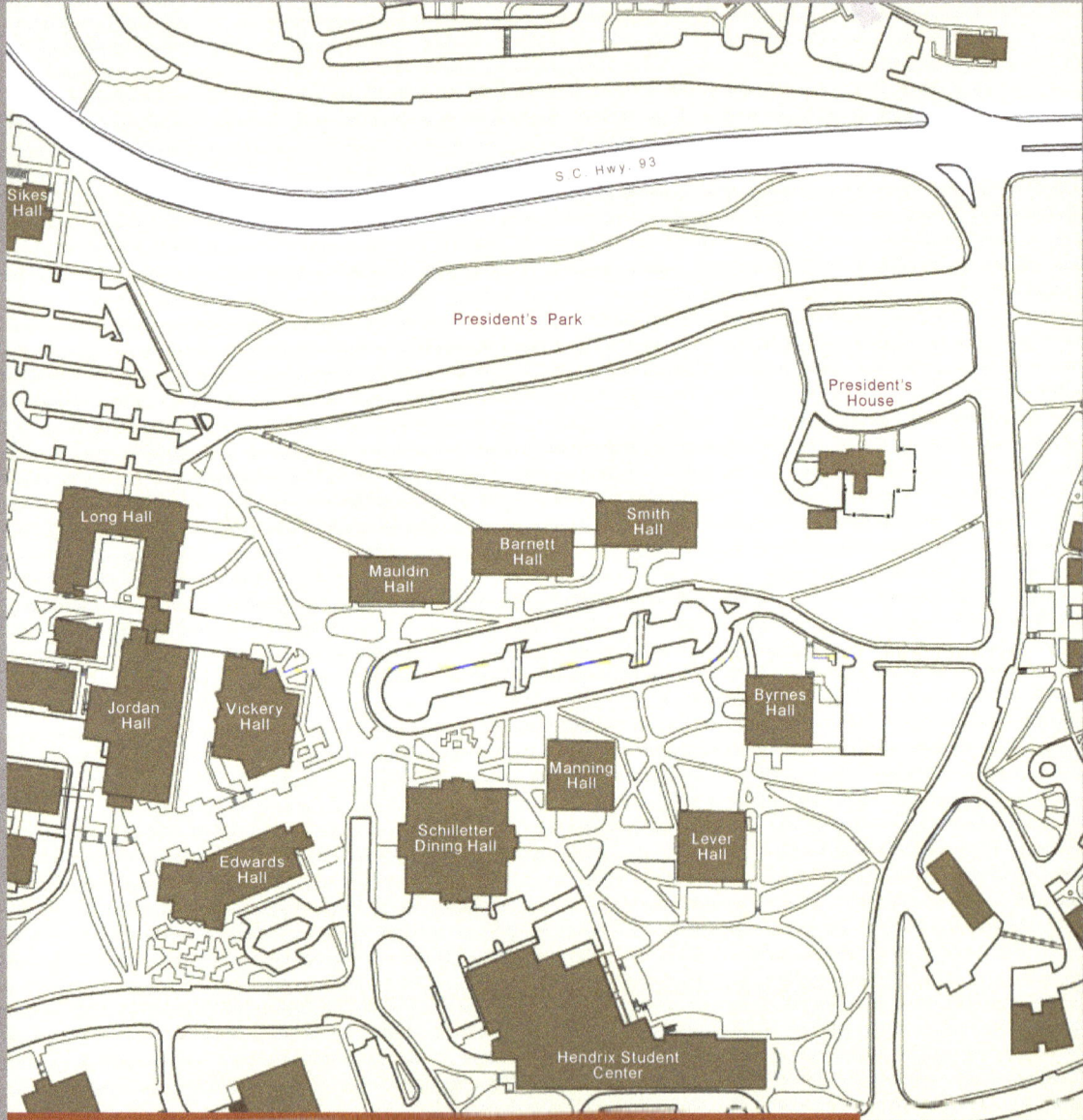

S.C. Hwy. 93

President's Park

President's House

Sikes Hall

Long Hall

Mauldin Hall

Barnett Hall

Smith Hall

Jordan Hall

Vickery Hall

Byrnes Hall

Manning Hall

Schilletter Dining Hall

Edwards Hall

Lever Hall

Hendrix Student Center

1/4 MILE, FOUR-MINUTE WALKING DISTANCE: 1,320 FEET

AREA FOUR
President's Park

P resident's Park, which stretches from Sikes Hall eastward to the President's House, was originally an area of native forest located on the Fort Hill plantation. Today it is part of the National Register of Historic Places District that includes Bowman Field and the Old Pecan Orchard.

President's Park is a good example of a managed green space that effectively combines several design objectives. It is a pleasant walking area for pedestrians as well as a typical habitat zone for campus wildlife. The vertical stratification of plantings creates multiple layers of vegetation from ground level to the tops of the tallest trees. This mixture of plant heights, coupled with a blend of deciduous and evergreen foliage, mimics native woodlands, even though the vegetation here is not nearly as dense as you would see in a natural forest. Nevertheless, the diversity of woody vegetation interspersed with areas of open turf provides a range of habitats that attracts squirrels, birds and insects.

ABOVE: **PRESIDENT'S PARK**
The entrance to President's Park begins near Sikes Hall. The park is part of a National Register of Historic Places District that includes several other sections of the Clemson campus.

LEFT: **CANOPY LAYERS**
Vertical layering of vegetation creates a mixture of foliage heights that increases its wildlife value.

TOP: **CAMPUS WALKERS**
Paths throughout the campus en-
courage walking and exploration.

BOTTOM: **FLAME AZALEAS**
Native flame azaleas provide early
spring nectar and pollen as well
as color!

ABOVE RIGHT: **ENTRANCE PATH**
Follow the brick pathway up
towards the President's Home to
explore President's Park and the
Old Pecan Orchard across Cherry
Road.

RIGHT: **SPRING SHOW**
The colors of spring abound in
President's Park, as represented
by these daffodils and azaleas.

From Sikes Hall, a decorative brick sidewalk leads up a slight grade towards the President's Home. A mixture of various large oak species, loblolly pines and magnolias surround the entrance to this walkway, sections of which are dedicated to specific graduating classes at the University. Amid low Japanese hollies are scattered beds of daffodils and azaleas that bloom in spring. Further along the pathway, native flame azaleas boast a bright Clemson orange against an early summer background of purple rhododendron flowers, where on sunny afternoons butterflies and bees gather nectar or pollen. Interspersed among the shrubs are ground covers of liriope, yew and turf, creating open space for foraging robins, mockingbirds, common grackles, and the ubiquitous gray squirrels. Holly and dogwood trees forming the mid-level canopy serve as an excellent source of late summer and winter food for birds.

ABOVE LEFT: **PATH AND SIKES HALL**
The brick sidewalk to President's Park begins at Sikes Hall which is flanked by Foster hollies.

TOP: **FLOWER AND BUMBLEBEE**
Rhododendron flowers are an important source of nectar and pollen for flower visitors.

BOTTOM: **ROBIN AND BERRIES**
Berries are a key source of wintertime food for birds such as the American robin.

LEFT: **FLAME AZALEAS IN SPRING**
Flame azalea flowers are favorites of honeybees, bumblebees, carpenter bees, and early hummingbirds.

TOP: **YELLOW-BELLIED SAPSUCKER**
Yellow-bellied sapsuckers drill rings of holes in the trunks of trees to gain access to the sap flowing beneath the bark.

ABOVE RIGHT: **PRESIDENT'S HOME**
The President's Home is surrounded by a traditional landscape.

LEFT: **SAPSUCKER HOLES**
Look for evidence of sapsuckers on maples and sweetgums throughout President's Park and the Old Pecan Orchard.

RIGHT: **SWEETGUM**
Look for the large old sweetgum near the road at the front of the President's House, recognizable by their star-shaped leaves. Sweetgum seeds are an important food source for over 20 species of birds, including cardinals and mourning doves.

Towards Long Hall, notice the rock streambed constructed to control storm water runoff at the lowest area of the park. Nearby wax myrtles and magnolias, along with rhododendrons and azaleas, not only provide spring color, but also serve as nectar plants for insects and seed sources for wintering birds. Large loblolly pines form a high canopy over this area. Listen for the calls of katydids and cicadas on warm summer nights. Look for the stone plaque dedicated to the Clemson students who gave their lives in combat during WWI.

The brick pathway winds past many large specimens of red, white, post and water oaks, along with more loblolly pines, hollies and magnolias. Notice the vertical layering of vegetation from the vinca at ground level, understory azaleas and clethra, mid-canopy dogwoods, redbuds, crepe myrtle and hollies, culminating with the upper canopy of oaks and pines. If you look beneath these large trees, you will see many fallen acorns and pinecones. Closer inspection will likely also reveal numerous small holes in the ground. These are stashing sites where the resident squirrel population hordes nuts and seeds for use as food during the winter and spring.

As you reach the eastern boundary of the park, marked by the intersection with Cherry Road, the white-columned President's Home is on your right. This 1950's replica of a southern plantation mansion is set against a border of stately magnolias that line the semicircular drive. Surrounding the well-manicured lawn are specimens of sweetgum, Japanese maple and sugar maple. Look closely at the trunk of the sugar maple located on the corner of the lawn nearest Cherry Road. The rings of small holes around the trunk were made by yellow-bellied sapsuckers. These woodpeckers drill holes to gain access to the sugary tree sap, which they use for food. Numerous types of insects are also attracted to the oozing sap. This in turn lures other bird species (including ruby-throated hummingbirds) that feed on those insects, forming a complex interdependency of plants and animals.

ABOVE: **SUMMER SONGS**
The repetitious nocturnal "songs" of cicadas are a familiar summer sound in President's Park.

TOP LEFT: **WWI STONE PLAQUE**
The stone plaque honoring World War I veterans is located near the dry stream bed, which handles storm runoff.

BOTTOM LEFT: **SQUIRREL STASHES**
Gray squirrels stash acorns and pine seeds in holes they dig in the open areas around oak and pine trees.

S.C. Hwy 93

Stone Gates

Old Pecan Orchard and Trustee Park

Newman Road

Cherry Road

Calhoun Courts
Apartment Commons

Thornhill Village
Apartment
Commons

Thornhill Village
Woods

Hunnicutt Creek Woods

1/4 MILE, FOUR-MINUTE WALKING DISTANCE: 1,320 FEET

AREA FIVE

*Old Pecan Orchard
and Trustee Park*

One of the last original remnants of Clemson University's early agricultural days can be found along the south side of SC Hwy 93 between Cherry and Newman Roads. The Old Pecan Orchard, also known as Trustee Park, contains a variety of fruit and nut trees whose present size suggests that at least some of them were planted in the early 1900's. These trees probably date back to around 1914, when the Smith-Lever Act first established the agricultural experiment station system in America. These trees thus represent one of the first attempts at a "demonstration" orchard in the Southeast. Twenty large pecan trees are still present in this area, along with oaks, maples, magnolias, dogwoods, crepe myrtles, deodar cedars, apples and other ornamental fruit trees. Today the area is maintained as a mixture of open turf, with an overstory of middle to tall trees that produce fruits and nuts of substantial food value to wildlife.

ABOVE: **PECANS IN WINTER**
The Old Pecan Orchard was planted during the early 20th century and is now home to extensive turf areas and many large pecan, oak and maple trees along with several other species whose fruits are important to wildlife.

pecan leaf

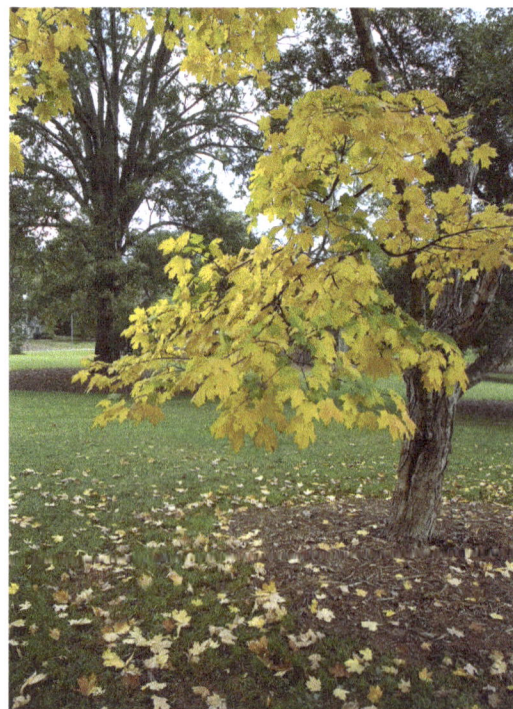

TOP: **PECANS**
When ripe, pecan fruits split open to reveal the familiar nut.

ABOVE RIGHT: **MATURE PECAN**
Pecans are native to the Midwest but have been successfully relocated to the South where they are now an important agricultural crop. The pecans in this area were likely planted 80-90 years ago by Clemson's agricultural experiment station as part of a demonstration orchard.

RIGHT: **MAPLES**
The brilliant fall foliage of red and sugar maple is one of the seasonal highlights of the Old Pecan Orchard.

Pecans are the most prominent trees here. Native to Midwest river basins, low spreading branches are characteristic of this cultivated species. With heights up to 140 feet and canopy spreads of 70 feet, pecans produce clusters of 3 to 11 fruits that ripen to reveal long, tasty nuts. In late fall, local residents can be seen picking loose nuts from the ground or tossing long, weighted ropes into these trees to shake down additional nuts. Search around the base of one of these old pecan trees and you will likely find a nut that has gone uncollected. Pecans are also an important component of the diet for campus gray squirrels, blue jays and American crows. Flocks of crows, often made up of related individuals, can frequently be seen in the Orchard working cooperatively to collect nuts and other foods. While most of the flock forages on the ground, others will stand guard in nearby trees to watch for potential predators such as hawks or feral cats.

Look for both sugar maples and red maples in the Old Pecan Orchard, identifiable by their characteristic palm-shaped leaves and striking fall foliage. Large white and red oaks are also present in the Orchard. These old trees are heavily colonized by mistletoe. Look up high in the crowns of these oaks, especially during late fall and winter when the leaves are absent, to see large clusters of mistletoe growing from the branches. Contrary to popular belief, mistletoe is not a true parasite. Instead, it is a green plant that photosynthesizes on its own but gathers moisture by extending its roots into the host's vascular system.

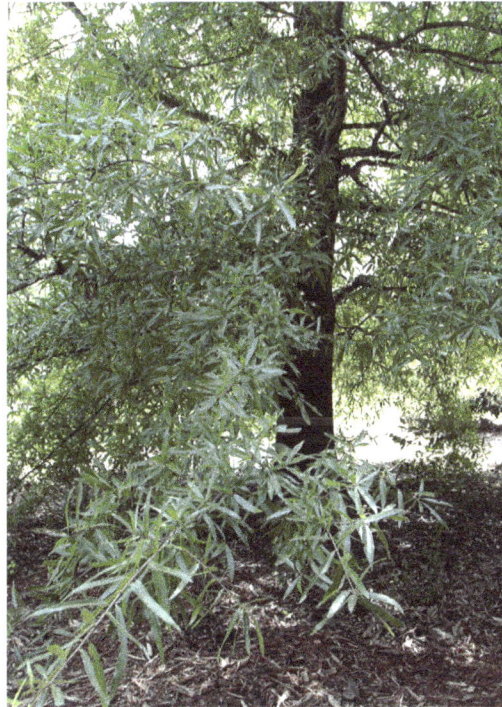

ABOVE LEFT: **CROW**
The American crow is a highly social bird that often forages in cooperative family flocks. Note the large body, jet-black coloration and distinctive "caw" vocalization of this bird.

TOP: **MISTLETOE**
Mistletoe is abundant in the highest branches of the oaks in the Old Pecan Orchard. Its white berries are consumed by a variety of fruit-eating birds. When the birds wipe their bills on tree branches after eating, they deposit the seeds in new locations favorable for growth.

BOTTOM: **WINDFALL APPLES**
A couple of remaining apple trees still produce tasty fruit.

LEFT: **OAKS**
White and willow oaks provide important habitat, nesting sites, and food for many birds.

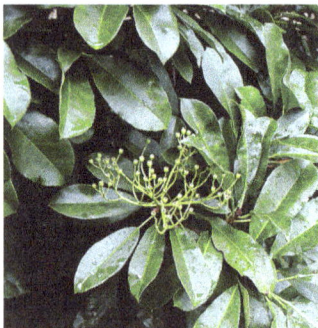

TOP: **FLOWERING PEARS**
Early blooming fruit trees, such as these pears near Calhoun Courts, are an important source of pollen and nectar for many spring insect species.

BOTTOM: **YOUNG REDTIP FRUITS**
Flower petals on this redtip have fallen off, revealing developing fruits.

ABOVE RIGHT: **PEAR TREES**
Look for the rows of the ornamental pears near the student housing area adjacent to the Orchard.

RIGHT: **REDTIPS**
The redtip on the right has a spreading canopy that reflects a more natural, dome-shaped form, compared to the pruned hedge (in decline) on the left.

During early spring, rows of ornamental pear trees burst into bloom near student housing at the end of Morrison Street closest to Cherry Road. These trees provide some of the very first reliable nectar sources for early insect species, and later will yield fruits used by birds and other animals. Oriental redtips line the eastern section along Morrison Street. This imported landscape species has been widely used as a hedge plant or privacy screen, but its popularity is waning due to its susceptibility to powdery mildews and the fireblight fungus. Compare the plants in these hedgerows to the large, dome-shaped specimen of redtip located among the daffodil beds nearest Cherry Road. This plant has not been pruned, thereby revealing a more natural, dome-shaped form. During early spring the dark green leaves serve as a contrasting background for clusters of small white flowers.

Although the turf areas of the Orchard are regularly mowed, there are nevertheless many examples of herbaceous plants that grow here. Some of these, like clover and the small purple violets that are common in spring, serve as browse for squirrels and rabbits, as well as important larval food sources for many species of insects, including sulfur butterflies. These open areas also provide good foraging habitat for robins, common grackles and other insect-eating birds that can be seen feeding there year round.

TOP: **ORANGE SULFUR**
Watch for small sulfur butterflies visiting flowers throughout the summer. Their caterpillars eat leaves of plants in the legume family.

BOTTOM: **CRAB APPLE FRUITS**
Ornamental crab apples are a source of fall fruit for a variety of wildlife.

ABOVE LEFT: **GRACKLE**
Flocks of common grackles make use of the open habitat found in the Old Pecan Orchard.

LEFT: **NUTRIENT-RICH LEAVES**
The tree canopy on Clemson's campus provides a significant resource for animals of all sizes. Consider the food source that the leaf biomass represents to herbivores large and small, as well as for the myriad decomposers and microorganisms!

ABOVE: **CONES**
Cryptomeria cones produce seeds that are attractive to some birds.

ABOVE RIGHT: **PLANTINGS**
Ornamental plantings around the stone gates create an attractive setting with layers of vegetation.

LEFT: **STONE GATES**
Four pairs of stone gates indicate entrances to Clemson's campus.

RIGHT: **DAYLILIES**
Daylilies are drought-tolerant, long-flowering, and reliable in southern climates.

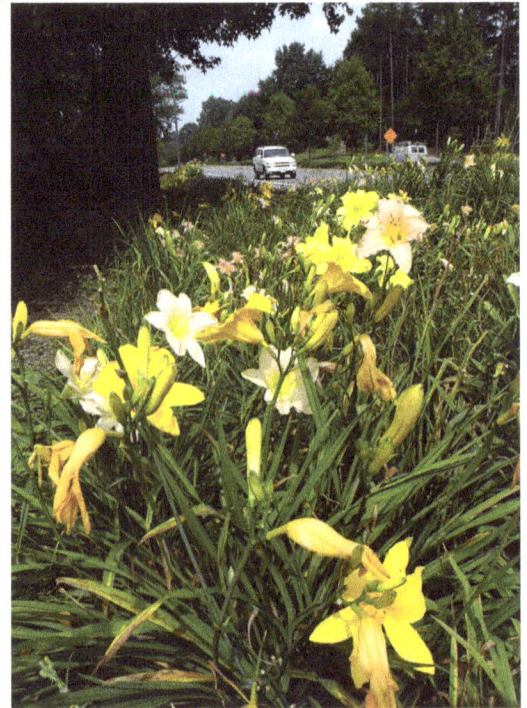

At the northeastern end of the Old Pecan Orchard are stone gates that frame the entrance to campus along Hwy 93 (also known as Walter Cox Boulevard). The gates are flanked by four large *Cryptomeria* evergreens against a backdrop of loblolly pine on one side of the road and hardwoods on the other. Also surrounding the gates are extensive beds of daylilies, bulbs and low-growing hollies. The stone gates that mark the eastern entrance to campus along SC Hwy 93 were a gift from the Class of 1928 and were moved to their current position for the University's centennial in 1989.

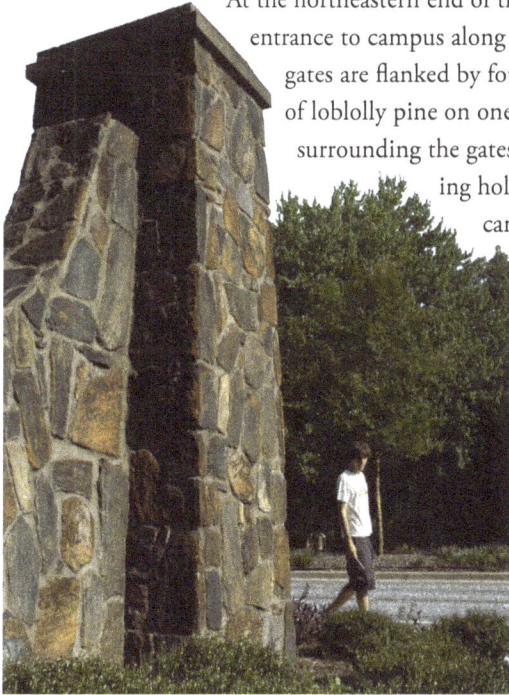

Cox Boulevard was recently enlarged into a four-lane divided highway and is now landscaped with beds of liriope and a row of ornamental street trees in the median. In combination with the stately old oaks and maples that are present along the road, it now takes only a bit of imagination to envision the tree-lined country lane that once served as the eastern entrance to the Fort Hill plantation.

TOP: **ARGIOPE SPIDER**
Garden spiders are at home in the ornamental plantings that line Cox Boulevard (Highway 93).

ABOVE: **HIGHWAY 93 MEDIAN**
Landscaped medians stretch from the Old Pecan Orchard to the beginning of President's Park.

ABOVE LEFT: **STONE GATES**
More recently installed stone gates echo the tradition of the original stone entrance gates to campus, on the road to Pendleton.

LEFT: **ORNAMENTAL PLANTINGS**
Zebrina and daylilies provide contrasting colors to the plantings around the gates.

RIGHT: **LANTANA**
Lantana 'Miss Huff' attracts hummingbirds, butterflies, bees, and other insects, as well as being winter-hardy in our climate zone.

Calhoun Courts
Apartments

Hunnicutt Creek Woods

Lightsey Bridge

Hendrix Student
Center

Hunnicutt Creek
Riparian Area

Lightsey Bridge
Apartments

South Carolina Botanical Garden

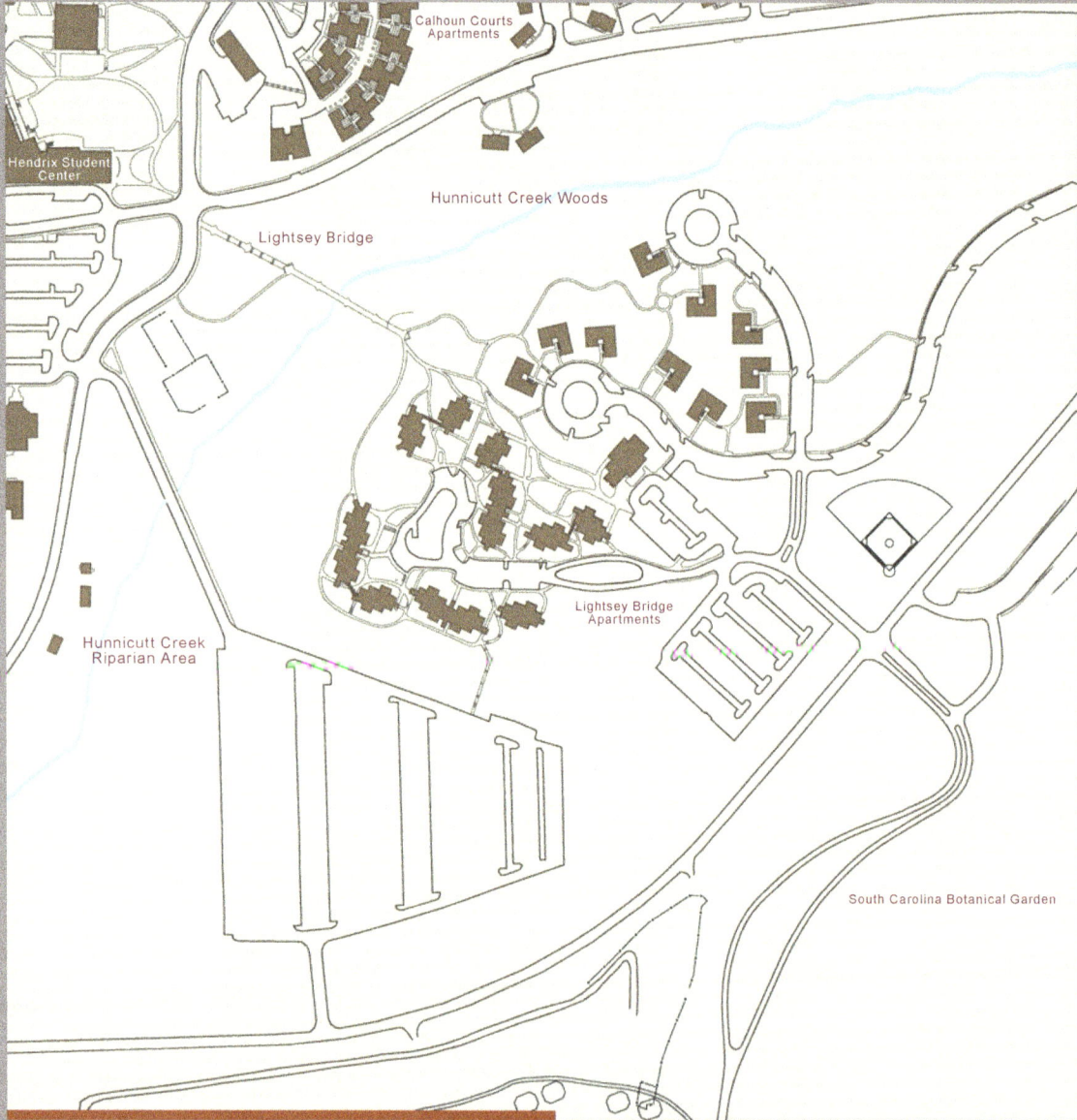

1/4 MILE, FOUR-MINUTE WALKING DISTANCE: 1,320 FEET

AREA SIX

Lightsey Bridge
Hunnicutt Creek Woods

The bridge to Lightsey Apartments provides excellent views into a mature hardwood forest and down onto the upper branch of Hunnicutt Creek. On the bridge, you're almost eye level with the canopy of native American beech, white oak, hickory and tulip poplar trees. An understory of sourwoods and flowering dogwoods add fall color, and magnolias and pines provide evergreen cover throughout the winter. Planted bald cypresses add additional plant diversity.

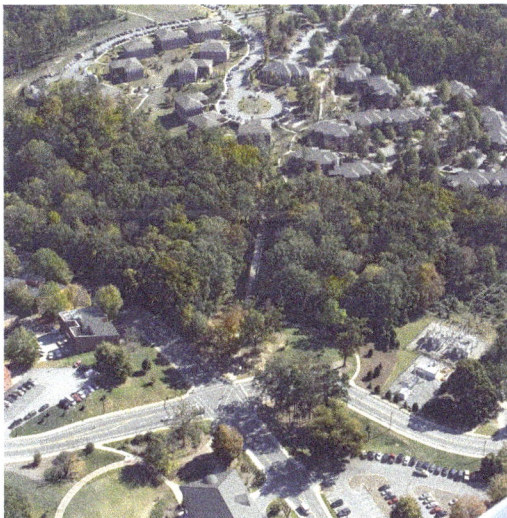

Though few people choose to walk through the woods on the ground, it is easily accessible along a sewer easement which is cleared and which can serve as a path for those seeking a closer view of wildlife on the forest floor. The creek bed reflects major erosion and gully formation that probably began during the years when this area was farmed. Watch for old fence posts and barbed wire, clues that suggest the area was once in pasture, perhaps grazed by sheep from the red sheep barn nearby. Erosion continues as the impervious surfaces of new apartments and parking lots increase runoff and silt deposition in the creek.

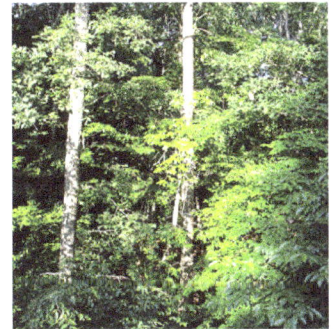

TOP: **CREEK VIEW**
Pedestrians enjoy an elevated view of a mature hardwood forest from the Lightsey Bridge.

LEFT & ABOVE: **FOREST VIEW**
A utility easement doubles as a path through the forest, which has been invaded with exotic plants including kudzu and silverthorn. Tall canopy trees include native white oak, American beech, and tulip poplar.

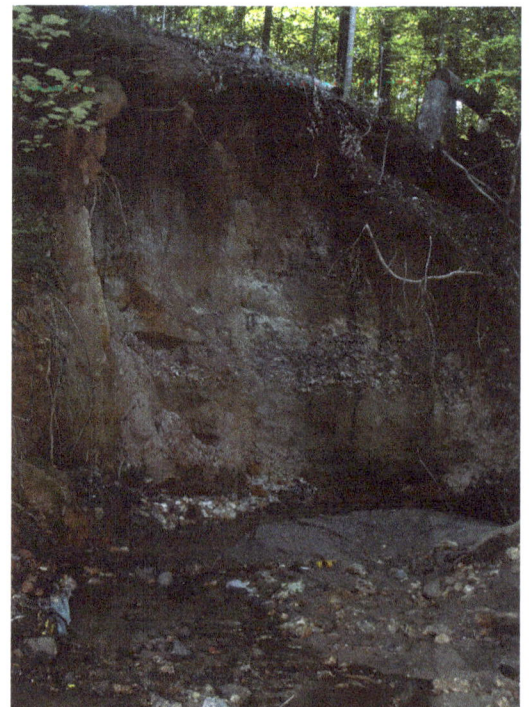

TOP: **LEAF-FOOTED BUG**
These large insects feed on a variety of plants, by sucking their juices. Note the flattened rear legs, thus their name.

BOTTOM: **DOGWOOD FRUITS**
Dogwood berries are rich in lipids, providing high-quality fats for wildlife.

ABOVE RIGHT: **MIMOSA**
The fine-textured mimosa tree is an invasive exotic which spreads along stream banks and on dry sites as well.

LEFT: **BRIDGE VIEW**
Many insects are well-camouflaged and do not leave the tree canopy.

RIGHT: **ERODED BANK**
Construction of parking lots and other impervious surfaces upstream exacerbate stream bank erosion problems that probably began when this area was farmed.

Some eroded cutaways along the stream bank provide shelter for animals, and the wide natural buffer serves as a wildlife corridor. These woods are home to many nocturnal mammals such as skunks, raccoons, opossums and fox. While these mammals are rarely seen during the day, bird activity is easily observed. Depending on the season, watch for territorial behavior, flocking, courtship, mating, nesting, and foraging. Bird diversity peaks during spring and fall migrations, and during the spring and summer breeding seasons. Birds take advantage of abundant insects in the woods, and a pair of pileated woodpeckers can often be heard working the lightning-damaged snags near the bridge.

Fruits and berries provide food as migrants move through the area eating and then dispersing seed over long distances. Bright red dogwood berries are eaten by 98 species of birds including flickers, downy woodpeckers, gray catbirds, brown thrashers, cardinals and white-throated and song sparrows.

The rough feel of these woods is enhanced by numerous treefalls, which create new spaces for succession to occur. Herbivorous millipedes, predaceous centipedes, and beetles can be found under fallen logs, and leaf litter is allowed to decompose naturally, contributing to nutrient recycling within the ecosystem. Both leaves and logs provide cover for reptiles and amphibians. Snakes, lizards, and turtles emerge on warm days, and salamanders may be found in areas moist enough to keep their skin damp and close to the creek, which provides the water necessary for reproduction. Carefully turn over a rock or log, and you may discover the hiding place of a cold-blooded animal.

The forest changes to open meadow as you near the apartments on the east side of the complex. As in old fields, a mix of annual, biennial, and perennial herbaceous plants can be found mixed with grasses and emerging woody species such as red cedar and tulip poplar. This is a great place to study old field succession. Come back and take a look over time as the "pioneer" species like broomsedge, ragweed, and goldenrod which initially cover the bare soil are overtaken by blackberries, loblolly and shortleaf pines. Eventually a subcanopy of shade tolerant dogwoods and sourwoods will become established under an overstory of oaks and hickories.

TOP LEFT: **RED-TAILED HAWK**
Red-tailed hawks hunt small mammals, birds, and snakes by day, whereas owls forage at night.

TOP: **NIGHT ANIMALS**
Nocturnal mammals such as skunk, fox, raccoon, and opossum inhabit these woods.

LEFT: **WOODPECKERS**
Pileated and other woodpeckers excavate cavities in dead trees, where they nest and raise young.

BOTTOM LEFT: **BEETLE**
A variety of beetles make their homes in forest habitats.

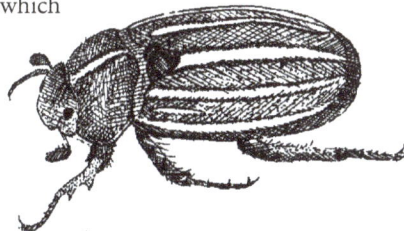

TOP: **INVASIVE ELEAGNUS**
Silverthorn is a fast-growing weedy ornamental that outcompetes native plants.

ABOVE: **GREEN ANOLE**
A male green anole signals for a mate by displaying his brightly-colored throat.

ABOVE RIGHT:
Edge environments where hardwood forests meet open meadows attract a wide variety of wildlife. The winter landscape reveals rolling topography and distant views of campus dormitories.

LEFT: **HONEYSUCKLE**
Beautiful but invasive, Japanese honeysuckle flourishes in southern climates.

RIGHT: **KUDZU**
Introduced from Japan in the early 1900's, kudzu is a deciduous vine infamous for its ability to grow out of control.

Queen Anne's lace is an attractive European wildflower whose flowers attract pollinators such as bees, syrphid flies, and butterflies. Predatory insects such as spiders feed on insects throughout the field and forest. Many insects are camouflaged and do not leave the canopy and are therefore difficult to observe. Katydids and leafhoppers look like leaves, and some spiders and beetles mimic bark, foliage, or flowers. All of these insects become part of the food chain, and the shrew that eats the katydid may eventually become a meal for top carnivores like the great horned owls or red-tailed hawks that inhabit these woods.

The woods are plagued by invasive exotic species including silverthorn, mimosa, Chinese privet, English ivy, kudzu, and honeysuckle. A dense stand of silverthorn and the steep topography make access to the creek difficult in many places.

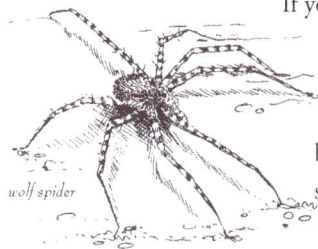

ABOVE LEFT: **WILD CARROT**
Queen Anne's lace (wild carrot) is visited by a variety of insects.

TOP: **PREDATION**
An earthworm makes a meal for a small garter snake.

ABOVE: **PAPER WASP**
Female paper wasps establish new colonies in spring, building open, papery nests.

If you are feeling adventurous, look for orb weavers under the bridge and aquatic insects in the creek. Orb weavers are spiders that spin complex radiating webs. The common garden spider creates a thick zigzag strand that may be an adaptation which improves the spider's ability to survive by warning birds and mammals of its presence. The warning saves the spider from having to expend energy rebuilding a destroyed web. She can efficiently go about the business of capturing and eating smaller prey instead.

wolf spider

If you are lucky, you may find a phoebe nesting under the bridge, or a territorial dragonfly may even land on your hat. If you're unlucky, one of the wasps nesting under the bridge or one of the many types of ants marching along under the walkway may warn you away. When you're back on top of the bridge, enjoy the sounds of the creek and the songs and sights of the warblers, catbirds, chickadees, and vireos that inhabit this rugged deciduous forest.

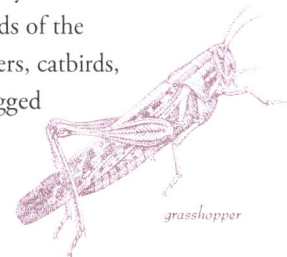

dragonfly

grasshopper

Thornhill Village
Apartments

Perimeter Road

Fire
Station

Lightsey Bridge
Apartments

Duck
Pond

Hayden Conference and
Nature Learning Center

Hanover House
and Heirloom
Garden

Horticultural
Gardens

Heritage
Pond

US HWY. 76

S.C. Botanical Garden

Heritage
Garden

Arboretum

Middle Branch of
Hunnicutt Creek

Wildflower Meadow

Butterfly Garden

Lower Branch of
Hunnicutt Creek

Piedmont Prairie

Discovery Center

Geology Museum

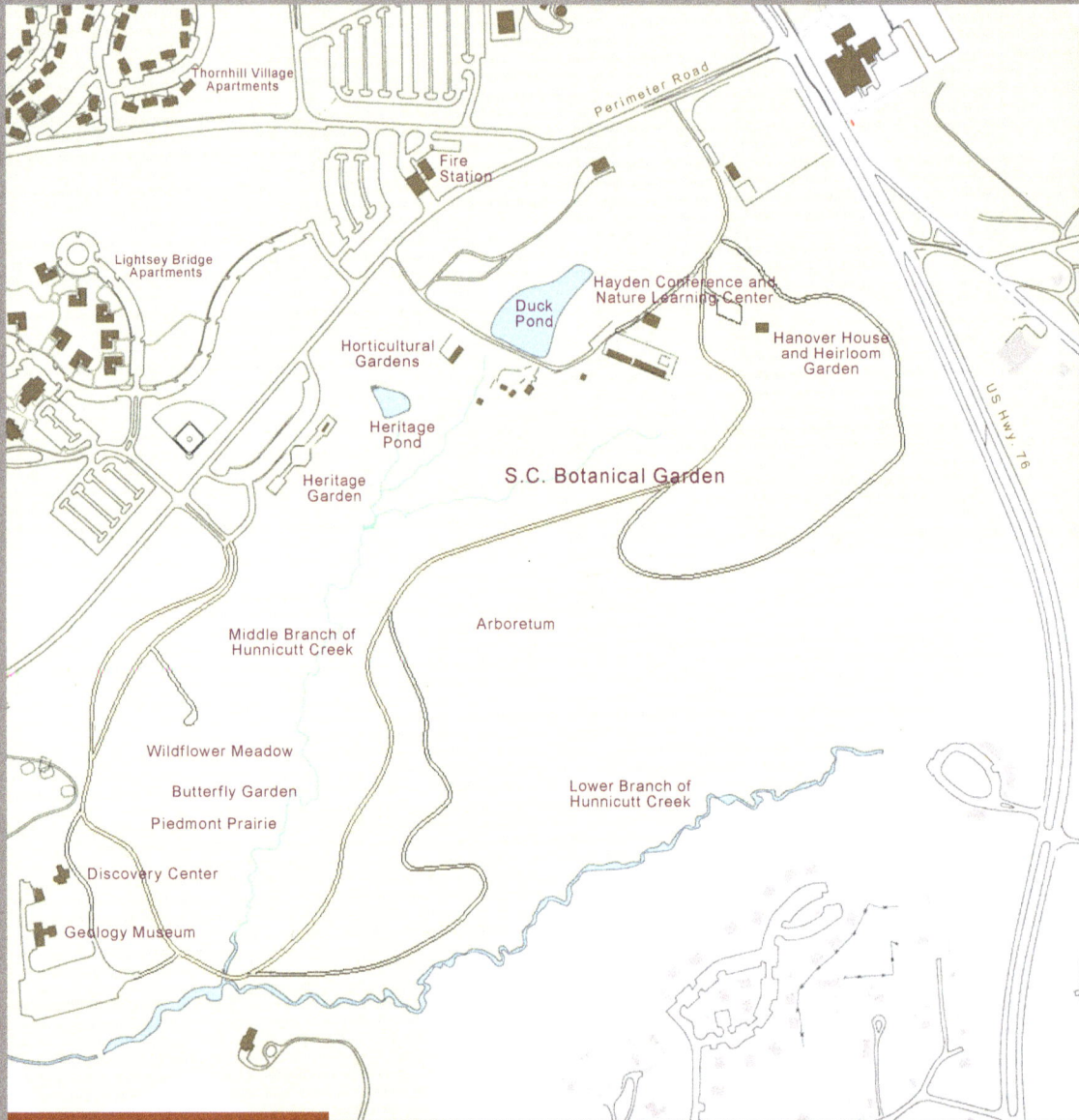

1/4 MILE, FOUR-MINUTE WALKING DISTANCE: 1,320 FEET

AREA SEVEN

The South Carolina Botanical Garden

The South Carolina Botanical Garden supports a diversity of plants and animals in its varied habitats. While you're visiting, enjoy observing the birds, insects, and other animals that live in the Garden as well as the diversity of native and ornamental plants!

The Horticultural Gardens near Pearman Blvd. (Perimeter Rd.) include some of the most visited Garden areas – the Hosta Garden, Wildlife Habitat Garden, the Display Garden, and the Xeriscape Garden. These established gardens include perennial beds, shrub plantings, and a variety of native and ornamental tree species which provide food and shelter for a variety of wildlife -- including insects, spiders, mammals, and birds.

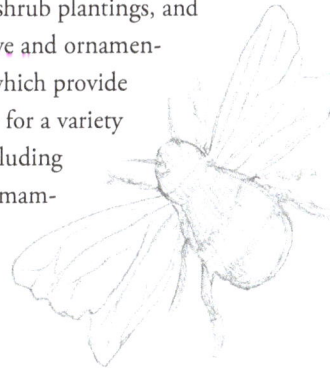

TOP: **WATERFALL**
The Hosta Garden and its waterfall provide a cooling respite on hot summer days.

ABOVE: **GARDEN SIGN**
Seasonal displays draw attention to the Garden's entrance sign.

The gardens near the Discovery Center and Geology Museum and the borders near the Hayden Conference Center and the Nature Learning Center are also lively with wildlife activity.

TOP: **HUMMINGBIRDS**
Ruby-throated hummingbirds are attracted to tubular red, orange, and blue flowers throughout the Garden.

ABOVE: **HONEYBEES**
Honeybees, native to Europe, favor the nectar-rich flowers of rosemary especially in cool times of the year, when other flowers are scarce.

ABOVE RIGHT: **CABOOSE**
The Caboose is a Garden landmark, surrounded by mixed shrub borders featuring tea olives, hollies, wax myrtles, and azaleas.

LEFT: **ARBORS**
Notice the variety of evergreen vines growing on the stone arbors near the Caboose, including clematis, Carolina jessamine, and crossvine.

RIGHT: **CROSSVINE**
In early spring, look for the beautiful trumpet-shaped flowers of our native crossvine.

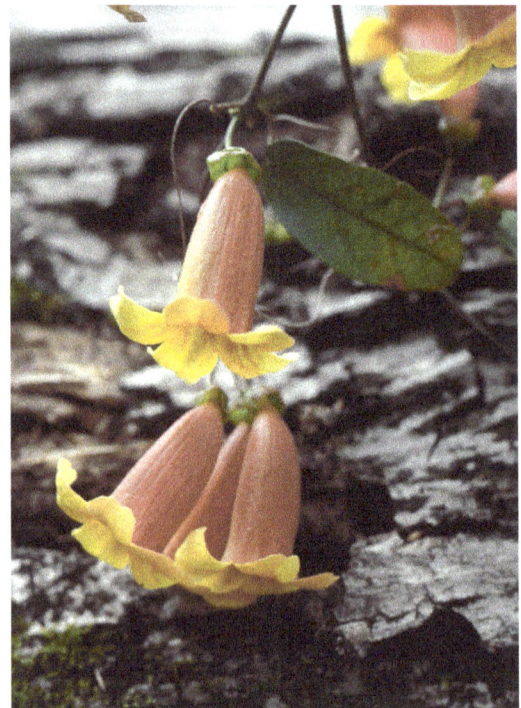

Many of the flowers in the ornamental beds throughout the South Carolina Botanical Garden provide nectar and pollen attractive to pollinators and other flower visitors. During the growing season, take a moment to watch bumblebees and honeybees foraging for pollen and nectar, and in the process, transferring pollen between flowers, producing energy-rich fruits and seeds. In addition, leaves and stems provide cover and food for a variety of other insects, which in turn provide food for a diversity of insect-eating birds. The rich organic soils and deep leaf mulch in garden beds and woodland areas team with soil organisms that recycle nutrients and contribute to the food chain and ecological balance of the Garden.

In the Garden's natural areas and woodlands, native trees and shrubs, interspersed with non-native plants both deliberately planted and "volunteers," provide habitat for a variety of wildlife. See how many different species of birds, mammals, and insects you can observe during your visit to these garden areas.

Before visiting the Horticultural Gardens and the Garden's natural areas, head to the Discovery Center for more information about what's in flower, current programs, and to pick up a map. While you're there, stop by the Geology Museum to learn more about the world beneath your feet!

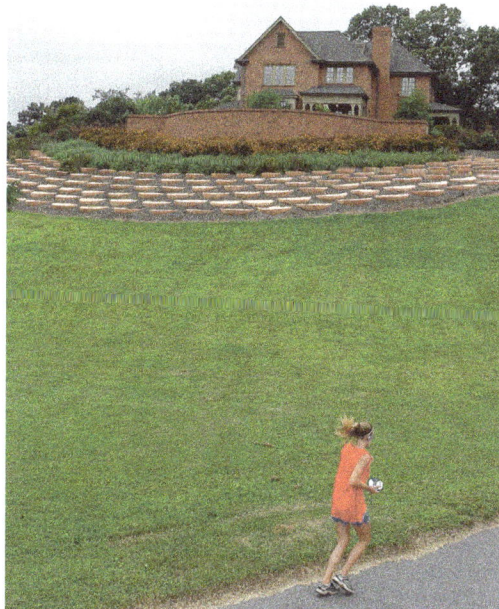

ABOVE LEFT: **EASTERN TOWHEE**
If you notice signs of movement in the leaf litter, check for the characteristic "kicking"of Eastern towhees and listen for the male's characteristic "Drink-your-tea" call.

TOP: **BEE BALM**
Monarda (bee balm) flowers are bumblebee favorites.

BOTTOM: **GEOLOGY MUSEUM**
The Geology Museum's perennial borders support chipmunks, squirrels, and birds, in addition to insects.

LEFT: **DAFFODIL DISPLAYS**
Daffodils flower in early spring throughout the Garden.

RIGHT: **GARDENS AND MEADOWS**
The Garden's Discovery Center is surrounded by diverse perennial borders, woodlands, and meadows.

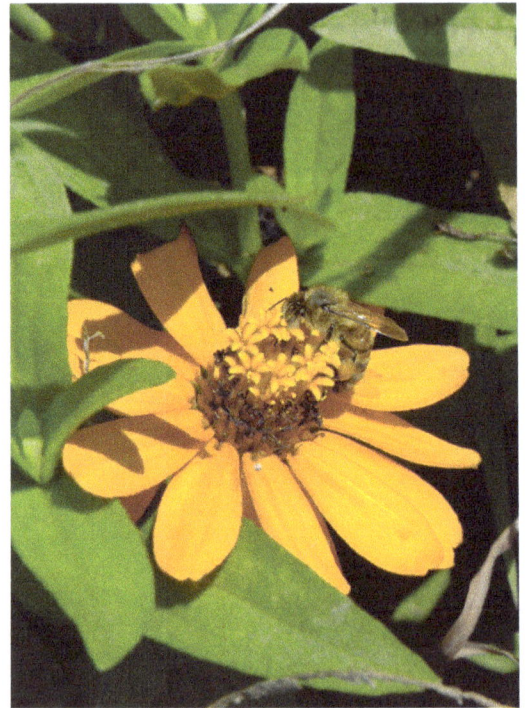

TOP: **EASTERN BLUEBIRD**
The Garden's bluebird boxes regularly house multiple broods of young bluebirds each spring and summer, supported by abundant caterpillars, beetles, ants, and spiders, as well as favorite fruits and berries.

ABOVE: **EASTERN CHIPMUNK**
Chipmunks are abundant in the areas near the Discovery Center and Geology Museum.

ABOVE RIGHT: **MEADOW FLOWERS**
Perennial black-eyed susans and zinnias provide nectar and pollen for foraging insects.

RIGHT: **BUTTERFLY GARDEN**
The Butterfly Garden stretches across the small hill opposite from the Discovery Center.

sharp-shinned hawk

The Discovery Center and Geology Museum garden areas are great places to watch for many kinds of wildlife. Hawks soaring over the meadows, bluebirds foraging for insects, and hummingbirds visiting *Salvia* flowers are frequent sights from spring to fall. Don't be surprised to see a chipmunk dashing into a nearby tunnel (look for a small, round, carefully maintained entrance for an active hole). In spring and summer, five-lined skinks are common around the stone and brick walls surrounding the gardens.

Look for the energetic activities of native bumblebees from spring to fall. Their thermoregulatory system and strong flight muscles allow them to fly at lower temperatures than butterflies. Only fertilized queen bumblebees overwinter (in abandoned rodent holes), reestablishing populations of working bumblebees each spring.

From the Discovery Center, the Butterfly Garden is a focal point on the top of the small hill across the meadow towards the forest edge. Designed to attract adult butterflies and support the life cycles of some common species, the Butterfly Garden teems with butterflies visiting lantana, butterfly bush, and other flowers from early summer to fall. Take a stroll to the Butterfly Garden to check out the diversity of butterfly species –swallowtails, monarchs, silver-spotted skippers, sulfurs, and blues. May through October are the best months to see adult butterflies, since most of our common garden species are present as adults only during warmer weather. Most species overwinter as eggs, caterpillars, or pupae, but a few species that survive the winter as adults may emerge on warm days, including sulfurs and mourning cloaks.

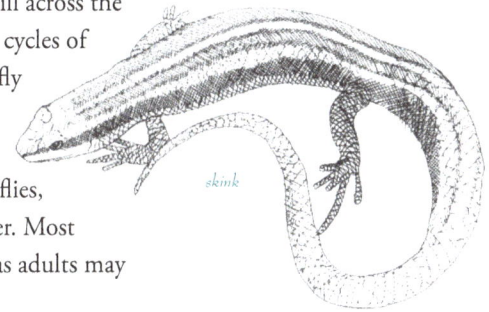
skink

TOP: **BUMBLEBEE**
Pollen baskets loaded with pollen indicate good foraging for this bumblebee.

TOP LEFT: **SHARP-SHINNED HAWK**
Sharp-shinned hawks and other raptors are commonly seen soaring above the Garden's meadows.

ABOVE: **SKINKS**
Five-lined skinks are commonly seen throughout the Carolinas near stone or brick walls, in rocky areas, and on logs.

LEFT: **TIGER AND JOE-PYE WEED**
Joe-pye weed is a favorite of Tiger swallowtails, bees, and other flower visitors.

RIGHT: **BUTTERFLY LIFE CYCLE**
Look for stages of the butterfly life cycle -- caterpillars and chrysalids are easiest to find. The pipevine swallowtail caterpillar is feeding on pipevine; the black swallowtail chrysalis is on fennel, a caterpillar host plant.

TOP: **PAINTED LADY**
Painted ladies are common garden butterflies. Honeybees are also attracted to purple coneflowers!

ABOVE: **BUTTERFLY WEED**
Butterfly weed is visited by over 30 species of insects and is eaten by monarch caterpillars.

ABOVE RIGHT: **MEADOW**
The Wildflower Meadow includes native species (such as monarda, blanketflower, and butterfly weed) and non-native species (such as cosmos).

RIGHT: **MEADOW VIEW**
The Garden's meadows include the native Piedmont Prairie, here under restoration, the Wildflower Meadow, and the open tall fescue meadows.

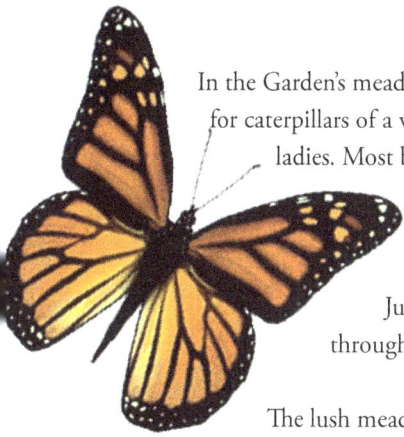

In the Garden's meadows grow plants (grasses and herbaceous species) that are hosts for caterpillars of a variety of other species, including buckeyes and American painted ladies. Most butterflies have relatively short lives as adults; monarchs are one prominent exception. The adults that migrate south in the fall to their Mexican overwintering sites live from 9 months to a year. Look for increased numbers of monarchs in our area during June and September, when their seasonal migration path brings them through South Carolina.

The lush meadow vegetation attracts meadow voles which eat stems, leaves, and flowers of grasses and perennials. Meadow voles construct elaborate systems of surface runways and underground burrows – look carefully and you may see evidence of their nocturnal grass-cutting activities. Eastern cottontail rabbits also frequent the Garden's grassy areas and lawns. Feeding on a variety of vegetation, cottontails take refuge in shrubby areas, or in old woodchuck holes in winter.

The ornamental Wildflower Meadow is managed for a showy display of wildflowers in late spring and early summer, and includes species from the western U.S., as well as eastern natives. The Piedmont prairie meadow (closest to the Discovery Center) is focused on native southeastern grasses and wildflowers, while the tall fescue meadows reflect the pasture heritage of this part of the Garden. An unwelcome reflection of that heritage is the high number of weed seeds that are part of the soil seed bank! The Garden's meadows reflect on-going management to encourage desirable species, while discouraging non-native weeds.

Hawks, owls, and vultures benefit from the diversity and abundance of small mammals and other prey that live in the Garden's meadows. The open edge habitats of the meadows also attract resident bluebirds.

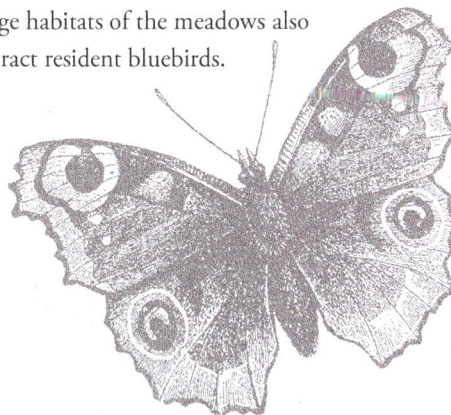

TOP LEFT: **MONARCH**
Monarchs are one of our most recognizable butterflies.

TOP: **HONEYBEE**
Honeybees take advantage of the nectar-rich flowers of butterfly weed.

ABOVE: **RABBIT**
Look for Eastern cottontails foraging for young shoots in grassy areas early in the morning or in the evening.

LEFT: **MEADOW HERBIVORES**
Meadow voles are abundant in grassy habitats.

RIGHT: **BUCKEYE BUTTERFLY**
Buckeyes are common in meadows.

TOP: **LUNA MOTH**
Luna moths are sometimes seen resting during the day, as they are normally only active at night.

ABOVE AND RIGHT: **HOSTAS**
Hostas are selected for their foliage diversity; in the Hosta Garden, they're displayed with other plants that do well in shade.

LEFT: **GARDEN BENCH**
The views from this secluded bench in the Wildlife Habitat Garden invite reflection. The evergreen and deciduous ferns planted along the streamside walk support a variety of insects and provide cover.

RIGHT **FLOWERING HOSTA**
Only a few hosta varieties are grown for their flowers, which can be very fragrant.

The Hosta Garden displays shade-loving plants – hostas grown for their foliage diversity and other plants that do well in medium light conditions. Look for hellebores in winter, daffodils and other bulb plants in spring, and the striking patterns, colors and shapes of hosta leaves in summer.

Heritage Pond, adjacent to the Hosta Garden, is SCBG's deepest pond. Its waters are home to aquatic larvae of many insects, including dragonflies, mayflies, and diving beetles, as well as native fish, such as minnow and bream. Ornamental carp, originally introduced to seal the pond's bottom, keep the water relatively muddy, but bright orange and white coloration and abundance make them frequently visible near the water surface. If someone is feeding the carp stale bread, watch their enthusiastic feeding behavior! At the entrance to the Wildlife Habitat Garden is a small grouping of butterfly and bee-attracting perennials bordered by a low stone retaining wall. The wall is a great spot to see green anoles, when the weather is warm.

The overstory of planted slash pine in the Wildlife Habitat Garden provides dappled woodland shade for a shady garden site enhanced for wildlife. A variety of berry-producing understory shrubs have been added along with evergreen shrubs essential for cover. Look for the bright red berries of deciduous hollies in winter or the attractive deep rose flowers of native rhododendrons in early summer.

TOP: **WINTERBERRY**
The bright red berries of this deciduous holly often persist into mid-winter, providing color, as well as late-season food.

ABOVE LEFT: **HOSTA GARDEN**
The Hosta Garden is recognized as an exemplary collection by the American Hosta Society.

LEFT: **EXPLORING...**
The Hosta Garden's paths invite exploration of the variety of leaf colors, textures, shapes, and sizes of hostas.

RIGHT: **POND AND BRIDGE**
Heritage Pond is a great place to look for turtles, bream, and other organisms as its depth supports a complex pond ecosystem.

TOP: **BUMBLEBEE**
Notice that this bumblebee is deep inside the salvia flower collecting nectar and pollen.

ABOVE: **NECTAR ROBBER**
In contrast, this carpenter bee is piercing the base of the flower, "robbing" the nectar

ABOVE RIGHT: **CHASTE-TREE**
The chaste-tree in the Xeriscape Garden provides pollen and nectar for foraging bees.

RIGHT: **DWARF CONIFER GARDEN**
The shapes and colors of these smaller conifers brighten winter landscapes and provide great cover for birds.

The Xeriscape Garden includes mixed shrub/flower borders, punctuated by a changing array of seasonal plantings, all designed for low water use. Notice the rosemary near the gazebo, the weeping yaupon holly, and large chaste-tree by the steps; all are drought-adapted species that do well without extra water. In summer, look for honeybee activity on the blue *Vitex* flowers –they'll be "buzzing" with bumblebees and honeybees collecting pollen and nectar.

A path winds its way through the Dwarf Conifer Garden, a collection of evergreen needle-leaved shrubs chosen for a diversity of shapes, colors, and textures. Don't expect all of these shrubs to be small; some of these cultivars are only small relative to the species' normal heights! Dwarf conifers are low-maintenance (no pruning required) and slow-growing, so are favorite choices for smaller landscapes and foundation plantings. Their foliage also provides excellent shelter for birds.

One of the oldest maintained niche gardens in the South Carolina Botanical Garden, the Flower Display Garden was laid out in the late 1970's. Enriched with annual additions of leaf mulch, these productive beds have been used in the past for trials of summer and winter annuals. Now, the garden displays a variety of flowering perennials in addition to seasonal annuals. From late spring to fall, look for interesting examples of flower shapes and colors and a variety of foliage colors and textures. These beds are frequently updated to showcase new introductions and landscape styles.

TOP: **DISPLAY GARDEN**
The Flower Display Garden beds feature a changing array of annuals and perennials.

ABOVE: **ST. JOHN'S WORT**
In the Xeriscape Garden, check out the variety of bees visiting St. John's wort flowers in late spring and early summer.

LEFT: **BLACK-EYED SUSANS**
Black-eyed Susans are drought-tolerant choices, here in the Xeriscape Garden.

RIGHT: **GARDEN PERENNIALS**
Perennial borders throughout the Garden change seasonally and are often updated or redesigned. Here swamp sunflower, ginger lilies, and Mexican bush sage are at their peak in late fall.

TOP: **CAMELLIA JAPONICA**
Camellia japonica flowers appear in late winter and early spring.

BOTTOM: **SASANQUA CAMELLIAS**
Camellia sasanqua cultivars flower in fall and early winter.

ABOVE RIGHT: **TERRACING**
Along the Camellia Trail, look for signs of the cotton-era terracing on the slopes above the path.

RIGHT: **DUCK POND KOI**
The orange ornamental koi were originally introduced to the Duck Pond and Heritage Garden ponds to help 'seal' the bottom surface. The koi have flourished, but they keep the pond waters muddy, due to their bottom-feeding behavior.

The South Carolina Botanical Garden began with a collection of camellias used for teaching. Once located near today's Memorial Stadium, they were moved to the site of the Camellia Trail in what once was a rubbish dump for Clemson College. Horticulture professor T. L. Senn was the Garden's founding director. Many additional cultivars have been added over the years (and the dump transformed into the garden and Duck Pond you see today). *Camellia japonica* (flowering in winter) and *C. sasanqua* (flowering in fall) are the primary species represented. Thousands of *Camellia japonica* varieties exist. If you're visiting from late fall to early spring, enjoy the hundreds of different cultivars in the Garden's collection. Notice the distinct terracing of the landscape in the Camellia Garden. It's thought that these are remnants of the extensive cotton terracing that was employed at Fort Hill by John C. Calhoun and Thomas Green Clemson, both progressive farmers for their time.

The Duck Pond and Heritage Pond were created in the 1970's during early Garden development. The Duck Pond, home to several resident mallards, white domesticated ducks, and a pair of Canada geese, is large and relatively shallow. Look for pond sliders basking on the banks and fallen logs in warmer weather. If you're lucky, you might see a Great blue heron or a green heron stopping by the Duck Pond.

The wood duck boxes placed on the pond edge have been very successful -- even though wood ducks are secretive and rarely seen, over 50 ducklings have been hatched in the Garden's boxes based on eggshell counts. Thirteen ducklings and their mother were recently spotted on an early spring morning making their way along the stream towards Lake Hartwell.

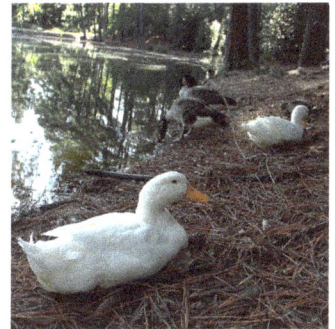

ABOVE LEFT: **GREAT BLUE HERON**
If you're lucky, you might see a great blue heron or a green heron stopping by the Duck Pond. Mallards are long-term residents.

TOP: **GARDEN TOAD**
Toads are common throughout the Garden! Look for them in summer and early fall in leaf litter and mulch.

ABOVE: **DUCKS**
The white domesticated ducks often pester visitors for a handout. It's better not to feed them, but if you do, cracked corn is better for them than bread or rolls.

LEFT: **CANADA GEESE**
Normally migratory, some Canada geese take residence in favorable spots, such as the Garden.

RIGHT: **WOOD DUCK BOX**
The wood duck boxes placed around Heritage Pond and the Duck Pond have supported a succession of wood duck broods.

TOP AND BOTTOM: **SEDUM**
Sedum 'Autumn Joy' attracts bees and butterflies in late summer. The umbrella-shaped flower clusters start faintly pink, then slowly deepen to dark rose, drying to an attractive brown in fall.

ABOVE RIGHT: **HUNT CABIN**
The Hunt Cabin overlooks an open grassy area and "dry stream bed" which handles overflow from the Duck Pond.

UPPER LEFT: **POLLINATOR BORDER**
The holly hedge frames the pollinator border near the Nature Center porch.

LOWER LEFT: **BUTTERFLY BUSH**
Butterfly bush flowers attract many butterflies, including this tiger swallowtail.

RIGHT: **RIVER BIRCH**
Our native river birch is widely planted because of its toughness.

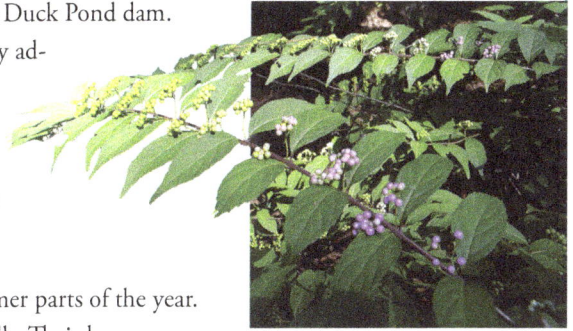

Enjoy the view of the Hunt Family Cabin from the Camellia Garden walk and the Duck Pond dam. The cabin was originally built in Seneca in the early 1830's. It has undergone many additions and transformations, including being entirely covered over by additional house framing. When the house was dismantled, the central cabin was moved and reconstructed on the main campus, and then moved to the Garden in the late 1970's. The Hunt Family Cabin is open for special heritage-related events and living history demonstrations on a seasonal basis.

Look for woodchucks foraging in the open grassy area in front of the cabin in warmer parts of the year. Woodchucks are sun-loving rodents, active morning and evening from spring to fall. Their burrows can extend to 30 feet long and up to 5 feet deep and, when vacant, are often used by other mammals such as cottontail rabbits and opossums.

As you walk up the hill towards the Hayden Conference Center and Nature Learning Center (on the lower level), enjoy the river birches and Japanese maples on the left. Near the entrance to the Nature Center, a mass planting of *Sedum* 'Autumn Joy' surrounds a crepe myrtle with an attractively sculptured trunk. For the past several seasons, several argiope spiders (garden or 'writing' spiders) have set up their webs among the sedum. Red-shouldered hawks have nested in the woods overlooking the duck pond in recent years; the open grassy areas beyond the Nature Center are favorite hunting grounds. You might spot a hawk carrying off a mouse or small snake for dinner!

The large holly hedge that frames the perennial plantings in front of the Nature Center provides excellent perching habitat for a variety of birds that enjoy the feeders. Look for the frequent visits of cardinals, chickadees, and tufted titmice, along with many others.

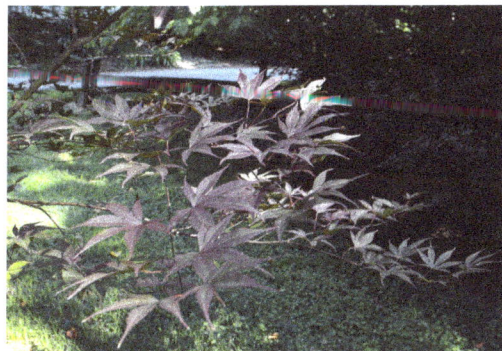

TOP: **BEAUTYBERRY**
The striking purple fruits of Chinese beautyberry are smaller than those of our native American beautyberry. Both are excellent landscape plants.

BOTTOM: **WOODCHUCK**
Woodchucks (also known as groundhogs) are herbivorous rodents, found throughout the Eastern U.S.

LEFT: **POLLINATOR BORDER**
The pollinator border features low-maintenance perennials that flower over an extended period, including purple coneflower and ironweed.

RIGHT: **JAPANESE MAPLE**
Japanese maples provide all-season interest, with attractive leaves, fall color, and sculptural form.

TOP: **TRILLIUMS**
Trilliums flower in early spring in rich woods and coves, and are planted in the Woodland Wildflower Garden.

BOTTOM: **CHRISTMAS FERN**
Look for the evergreen fronds of Christmas fern throughout the Garden.

ABOVE LEFT: **WOODLAND PATH**
The Garden's streamside and woodland paths support ferns and other shade-loving plants.

ABOVE RIGHT: **MEDITATION GARDEN**
The stream continues past the Meditation Garden all the way to Lake Hartwell.

RIGHT: **NATURAL DIALOGUE**
Look for one of the Garden's nature-based sculptures near this stream bend.

Beyond the Hunt Cabin, the Garden's woodland trails wind through largely forested areas harboring an abundance of wildlife.

Closest to the Hunt Cabin, the Woodland Wildflower Garden is at its peak in early spring, when the spring ephemerals (which flower before the trees leaf out) are at their peak. Oconee bells, trout lilies, bloodroot, foamflower, Atamasco lilies, and trillium are among the showiest flowers, but wild gingers, mayapple, native irises, and native azaleas are equally striking.

Native ferns are also abundant throughout the woodland areas. Look for New York fern, maidenhair fern, Christmas fern, and other native species.

Farther along the main trail next to the stream, you'll pass the Meditation Garden, recognizable by its gazebo. Distinctive boulders mark the site of Natural Dialogue, one of the Garden's nature-based sculptures. After crossing the power line opening, you will arrive at the Beech Grove. The beeches here are the largest in the Garden.

The forested areas of the South Carolina Botanical Garden are home to many woodland species, including eastern box turtles, barred owls, and woodpeckers. Characteristic second-growth oak-hickory forests, these areas exhibit different disturbance and recovery patterns.

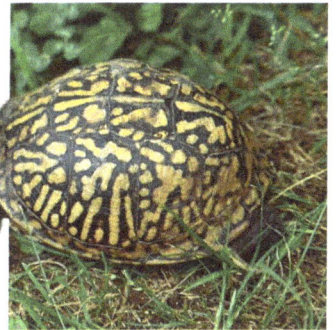

The Gwen Heusel Nature Trail loops through the most representative oak-hickory forest in the Garden. The dominant trees include white oak, red oak, tulip poplar, red maple, and mockernut hickory. Look for tracks of white-tailed deer and wild turkey in this part of the Garden.

Raccoons, yellow-bellied sapsuckers, and pileated woodpeckers frequent the larger forested areas, as do other woodland species such as screech owls and big-eared bats.

Pause quietly along any of the Garden's woodland trails and you may be surprised at what you see or hear! The Schoenike Arboretum encompasses much of the "back" area of the Garden. The Arboretum, founded by forestry professor Roland Schoenike, includes tree species and cultivars that do well in our climate zone.

TOP: **SNAG**
Cavities in dead or dying trees provide valuable nesting habitat for woodpeckers and other birds.

UPPER LEFT: **WOODPECKER**
Red-bellied woodpeckers feed on insects, berries, fruits, and nuts.

ABOVE: **BOX TURTLE**
Eastern box turtles live in forested habitats, thriving on a wide variety of plants and small animals.

LEFT: **SYCAMORE**
The camouflage-like bark of the sycamore is a common sight along campus streams and low areas.

Fort Rutledge Woods

Lake Hartwell Dikes

Fountain Pond

Lake Hartwell

Madren Center

Southern Green

Martin Inn

Walker Golf Course

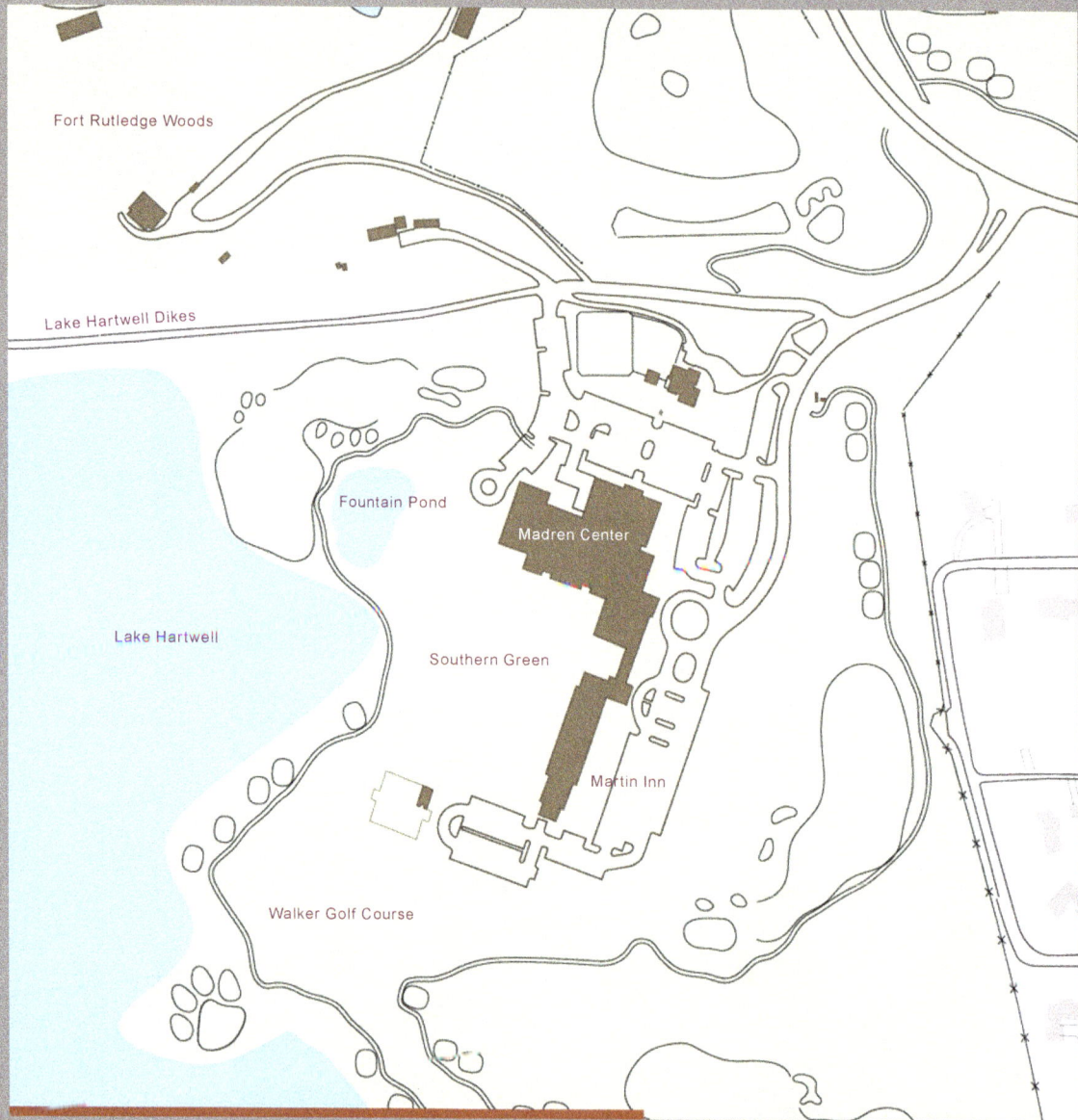

1/4 MILE, FOUR-MINUTE WALKING DISTANCE: 1,320 FEET

AREA EIGHT

Madren Center
Martin Inn
Lake Hartwell Dikes
Walker Golf Course

The Madren Center's location on Lake Hartwell provides lake views, access to the south dikes and the site of historic Fort Rutledge. The landscaped grounds surrounding the Center and the Martin Inn will harbor more wildlife species as they mature. Look for the striking groupings of purple-flowered chaste-trees in early summer near the entrance drive. These flowers attract a variety of bees and other visitors with abundant nectar and pollen.

A stroll along the south dike takes you past the fountain pond and along the lake's edge. The dikes were created in the early 1960's to protect Clemson University's historic agricultural land from the waters of newly created Lake Hartwell. A short trail off to the right leads to the site of Ft. Rutledge, an early military outpost located on the Seneca River.

The dike's vantage point provides a great place to look for water and shorebirds, as well as a variety of other wildlife. If the season is right, enjoy the purple martins energetically capturing insects in the vicinity of the martin house near the pond.

TOP: **MARTIN INN LANDSCAPE**
Landscaped plantings of lantana and Mexican bush sage are alive with insect visitors until frost.

BOTTOM: **TIGER PAW HOLE**
The signature hole of the Walker Golf Course borders Lake Hartwell.

TOP: **PURPLE MARTIN**

Martins are seasonal migrants, arriving here by mid-March or early April. They show strong site fidelity, returning to the same site year after year.

BOTTOM: **BULLFROG**

Bullfrogs are the largest frog in North America, often found living in warm shallow water. Listen for their "jug-o-rum" call in summer.

ABOVE RIGHT: **CAMPUS VIEW**

Tillman Hall is surrounded by trees in this fall view.

RIGHT: **LAKE HARTWELL DIKES**

Shorebirds take advantage of emergent vegetation along the south dike.

If you're lucky, you might spot a great blue heron wading in the shallow water hunting for food in the renovated wetland area past the pond. They hunt by standing still and waiting to strike passing fish. Shoreline trees provide a perch for kingfishers scouting their prey, small fish, crustaceans, and sometimes even insects. Watch for them along the water's edge.

Near the water treatment plant, the pockets of vegetation and surrounding woods provide habitat for small mammals and birds. The delicious fruits of native persimmons attract small mammals when they're ripe; look for the black persimmon seeds along the path left by nighttime foragers such as raccoons. A bit further on, the views include looking down towards the "Bottoms" (Calhoun Field Laboratory) and the aquaculture research ponds.

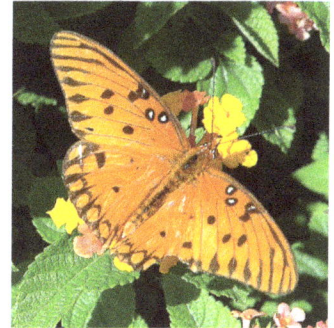

TOP: **LONG-TAILED SKIPPER**
The many species of skippers are challenging to identify, even for experts. An easily recognized common species is the long-tailed skipper, shown here visiting lantana flowers.

BOTTOM: **GULF FRITILLARY**
These colorful butterflies migrate north in successive broods from frost-free areas, tracking the emergence of their caterpillar host plants (passion vines).

ABOVE AND LEFT: **WALKER GOLF COURSE**
Diversity of landscape plantings increases the wildlife value of golf courses. A mixture of evergreen and deciduous trees, with natural area patches, improves habitat quality.

Dike

Fike
Recreation Center

Jervey
Athletic Center

Littlejohn
Coliseum

Clemson
Memorial
Stadium

Intramural Practice
Fields

Kingsmore
Baseball
Stadium

East Beach

Intramural Practice
Fields

Woodland
Cemetery

Practice Football
Fields

Lake Hartwell

Dike

Calhoun Field Laboratory

Old Seneca
River Lagoons

Aquaculture Ponds

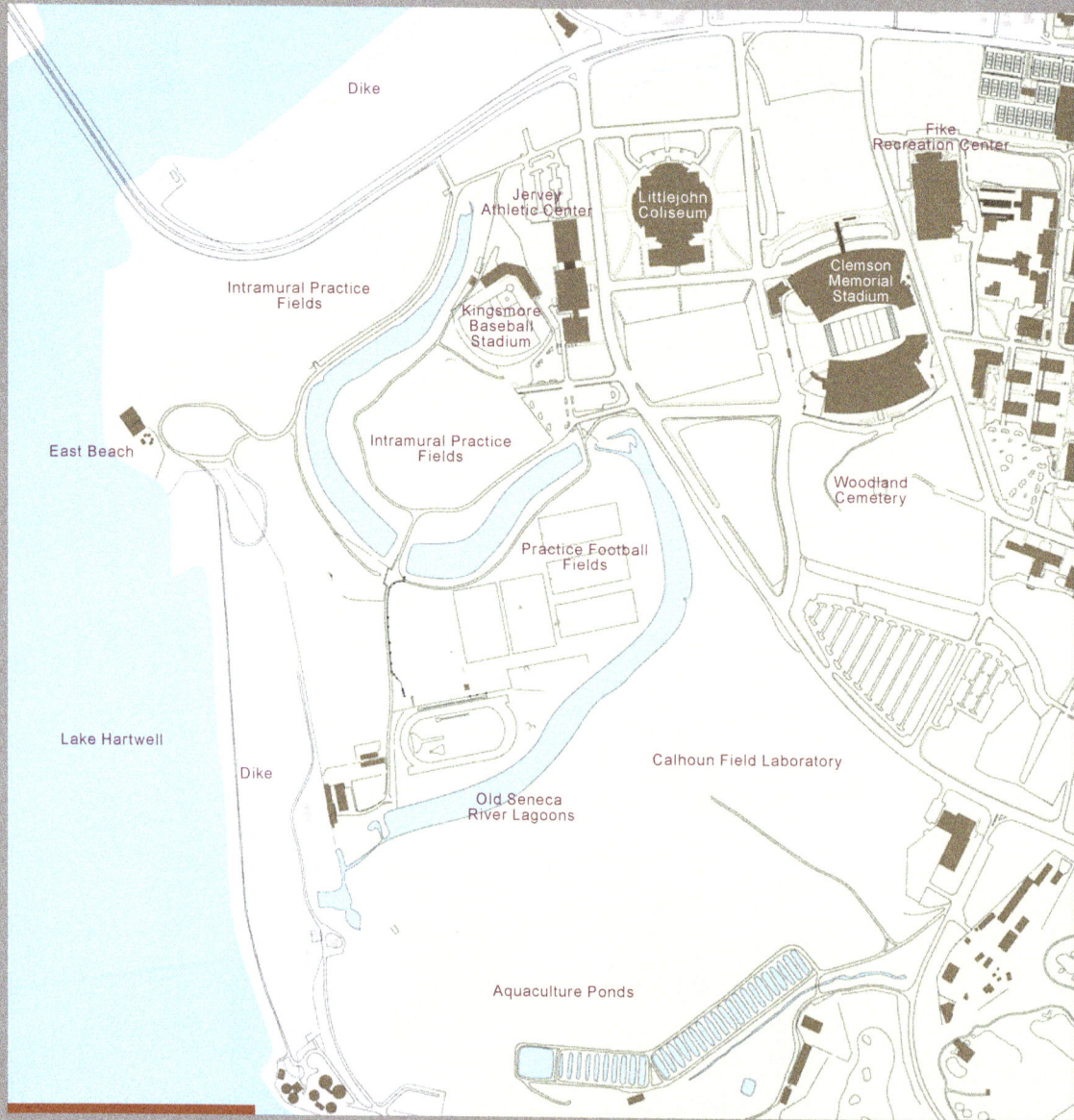

1/4 MILE, FOUR-MINUTE WALKING DISTANCE: 1,320 FEET

AREA NINE

The Woodland Cemetery
Lagoons and East Beach
The "Bottoms" (Calhoun Field Laboratory)

The Woodland Cemetery, also known as Cemetery Hill, is one of the highest and most historic points on campus. The wooded knoll is a quiet place where large trees shade a sacred site. Names like Sikes, Poole, and Fike, familiar because they grace the facades of buildings on campus, are etched into gravestones beneath guardian oaks, pines and poplars.

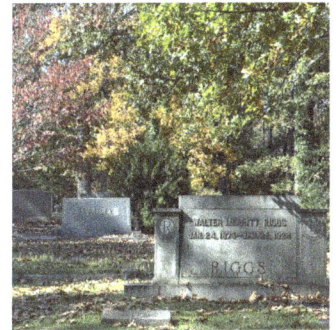

Smaller native hilltop species like blackgum and sourwood add fall color among the scarlet oaks, post oaks, black oaks, and southern red oaks.

The Woodland Cemetery was named and approved by the Board of Trustees in July of 1924. Clemson's president Walter Merritt Riggs first proposed the idea of having a cemetery for faculty in 1922, and the site of the old Calhoun cemetery above the Seneca River was chosen.

ABOVE: **CEMETERY HILL**
The Woodland Cemetery's oaks, hickories, maples, dogwoods and blackgums provide lovely fall color. Camellia flowers add pink and white in fall and early winter.

LEFT: **THE "BOTTOMS"**
The old Seneca River lagoons meander through the athletic fields and along the "Bottoms" below the Lake Hartwell dam. Cemetery Hill's protected tree cover is visible east of the stadium.

TOP: **OLDEST GRAVE**
*The oldest known grave (1837)
in the Woodland Cemetery lies beneath the shade of an Eastern red
cedar in the Calhoun family plot.*

ABOVE RIGHT: **ENTRANCE**
*Eastern hemlocks frame the en-
trance to the Woodland Cemetery.*

RIGHT: **CEMETERY GATES**
*Fifteen members of the Calhoun
family are buried in the family
plot, enclosed with a stone and
wrought iron fence on the peak of
Cemetery Hill.*

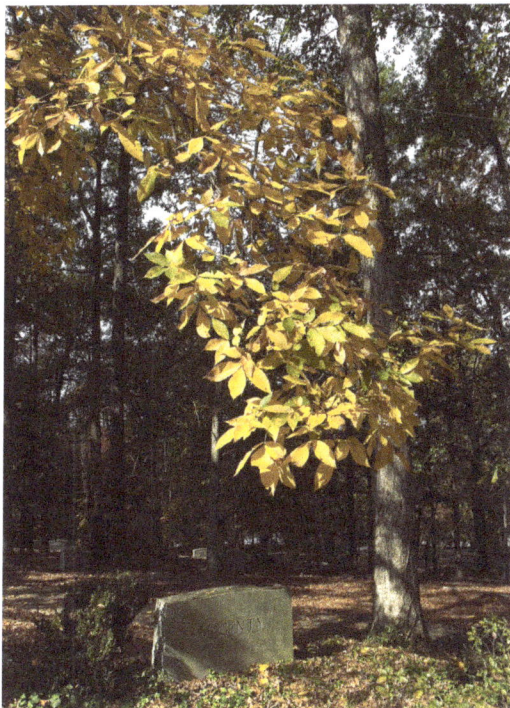

Shade loving Canadian or Eastern hemlocks flank the entry gates to Cemetery Hill. This fine-textured evergreen has a graceful pyramidal form and the small terminal cones are a favorite in wreaths and floral arrangements. Like the Eastern red cedar also found on this site, this native evergreen provides good cover for birds and other wildlife on top of the hill, where wind speeds are often higher. Hemlocks are threatened by the hemlock woolly adelgid, an introduced pest, which eventually kills the tree.

A buffer of trees surrounds the cemetery, and in the spring, you can see the white flowers of dogwood and serviceberry. Many birds and animals enjoy the sweet, juicy summer fruit of serviceberry, which was eaten by the Cherokee long before the first grave appeared on Cemetery Hill.

TOP: **EASTERN HEMLOCK**
Seeds in the small brown cones of Eastern hemlock are favored by finches, chickadees, and other seed-eating birds.

ABOVE LEFT: **FALL COLOR**
The clear yellows of hickories and maples reflect carotene and xanthophyll pigments unmasked by the loss of chlorophyll in senescent leaves.

LEFT: **CEMETERY HILL**
Seen here from the "Bottoms", the Woodland Cemetery hilltop and its buffer of trees is clearly visible. This area has been designated for protection as open green space with historic value in the campus master plan. Wading birds visit the aquaculture ponds in the foreground, competing with researchers for the fish and shrimp grown in the ponds.

TOP: **BELTED KINGFISHER**
Watch for kingfishers perching along the water's edge.

ABOVE: **SASSAFRAS SAPLING**
The mitten-shaped leaves of sassafras are characteristic of this native tree which has three different leaf shapes.

ABOVE RIGHT: **LAGOON**
This basin is a remnant oxbow lake formed by the Seneca River and modified over the years.

RIGHT: **CALHOUN FIELD LAB**
Aquaculture ponds and experimental vegetable and grain fields occupy the last area of historic agricultural lands on campus.

TOP: **BERRIES**
Fleshy fruits are often sugar-rich when ripe, providing energy for mammals, birds, and other wildlife. Their colors change when ripe, signaling that they're ready to eat!

ABOVE: **CROPS**
The Calhoun Field Laboratory supports research evaluation of grains and other crops, in addition to organically produced vegetables and flowers.

LEFT: **RIVER BIRCH IN WINTER**
The interesting bark texture and branch structure of river birch can be clearly seen in winter.

RIGHT: **LAGOON EDGE**
Deciduous trees near the lagoons provide seasonal habitat for resident birds, as well as migrants.

ILLUSTRATION CREDITS

Top (T)

Above Left (AL) Above (A) Above Right (AR)

Left (L) Right (R)

Bottom (B) Below Left (BL) Below Right (BR)

56 T (Lisa Wagner); B (Tim Spira); AR (Umit Yilmaz); L (Mary Haque); R (Lisa Wagner)

57 Birds (Clipart.com); T (Clipart.com; red fox, USFWS Digital Library System); beetle drawing (Cindie Brunner)

58 T, AR, R (Umit Yilmaz); A (Clipart.com); L (Tim Spira)

59 Drawings (Dover); AL (Mary Haque); T (Clipart.com); A (Russ Ottens, University of Georgia, Forestry Images)

61 T, L, A (Umit Yilmaz); drawing (Lisa Wagner)

62 T (from Early Birds, by Minnie Miller and Cyndi Nelson, Johnstone Books); A, L (Lisa Wagner); AR (Umit Yilmaz); R (Tim Spira)

63 AL (Clipart.com); T (Lisa Wagner); A, R (Umit Yilmaz); L (Mac Sprott)

64 T (USFWS Digital Library System), A (Clipart.com); AR (Tim Spira); AR, R (Umit Yilmaz)

65 Drawings (Cindie Brunner); T, L, R (Lisa Wagner)

66 T, A (Lisa Wagner); AR (Mary Olien); R (Umit Yilmaz)

67 TL, A, L (Clipart.com); T (Lisa Wagner); drawing (Cindie Brunner)

68 T (Tim Spira); AR, L, R (Umit Yilmaz)

69 AL (Lisa Wagner); T, L, R (Umit Yilmaz)

70 T, A (Lisa Wagner); AR, R (Umit Yilmaz)

71 T, A (Lisa Wagner); L & inserts (Umit Yilmaz); R (CU Photographic Services)

72 T (SCBG); AR, R (Umit Yilmaz)

73 AL (Gene Oleney, Fermilab); T (Lisa Wagner); Mallard (USFWS Digital Library System); A, L, R (Umit Yilmaz)

74 T, AR, UL (Lisa Wagner); A, LL, R (Umit Yilmaz)

75 T, R (Umit Yilmaz); A (Ed Pivorun); L (Lisa Wagner)

76 T, A (Tim Spira); AL, AR, R (Umit Yilmaz)

77 T (Tim Spira); UL, A (Clipart.com); L (Umit Yilmaz)

79 T, B, L (Umit Yilmaz)

80 T, R (Mary Haque); B, AR (Umit Yilmaz)

81 T, A, L (Umit Yilmaz)

83 A, L (Umit Yilmaz)

84 T, R (Umit Yilmaz); AR (Vic Shelburne)

85 T, AL, L (Umit Yilmaz)

86 T (Clipart.com); AR (Mary Haque); A, R (Umit Yilmaz)

87 T, A, L, R (Mary Haque)

Campus area maps were created by Umit Yilmaz using digitized Clemson University maps from University Facilities.

Every effort has been made to attribute photos and images used in this field guide. Images and illustrations were used with permission of the photographer, illustrator, publisher, or according to the permissions regulations of the source. Images and photos obtained from Clipart.com are the copyrighted property of JupiterImages Corporation and are being used with permission under the license agreement.

INDEX

www.ingramcontent.com/pod-product-compliance
Lightning Source LLC
Chambersburg PA
CBHW061224270326
41927CB00025B/3489